By My Bootstraps

A Journey Through Grit, Grace, and Gratitude

Debra Downey

Table of Contents

A Tale Of Two Grandmothers

Sandra Bean was born a classic blonde beauty who would grow into an intelligent, curvaceous spitfire of a woman. Iowa in the 1940s was not a place for an intelligent woman, though, and Sandy eagerly jumped into married life at the age of seventeen. Unfortunately, for everything that she had going for her in the looks and intelligence department, Sandy's taste in men was far lacking. Her choice for a first husband was a man named Gene McCauley, a tall sailor with a toothy grin and a passion for women. Marriage made an honest woman of Sandy, but it did little to slow down Gene's fun with the ladies.

Gene was not Sandy's only suitor. She had caught the eye of another young sailor, a man named Jack, who had become best friends with her brother after leaving the Navy. Sandy didn't trust this boisterous man with a crooked smile, and she kept her heart with Gene. Jack would tease her often, "when are you going to leave that no-good squid and come home with me?" But she had faith in her man and kept the home fires burning while he sailed the world over.

It was a loyalty that would break her heart.

Sandy was pregnant with her third son when she got an unsettling telegram. "Got a girl in trouble in Japan. Need money. Sell your wedding ring. Gene."

My granny sent a furious message back:

"No babies are dying by my wedding ring. Find your own money. And don't come home. Sandy."

But Gene came home anyway, charming as ever and begging for forgiveness. It was a mistake, it won't happen again, and he loves his boys. Amends were made.

Gene stayed for two weeks, then told his wife that he had orders to leave once again. They said their goodbyes, and Sandy tended to her three young boys.

Another month went by, and Sandy learned that she was pregnant again. She had decided to keep her news to herself for a little while to tell Gene first. Soon after discovering her news, she was shopping in town and sighted a familiar tall man, with his arms wrapped around a woman with a bulging belly. Not one to avoid confrontation, Sandy bolted down the street and right up to the couple to confirm what she thought she saw.

"Gene McCauley, what exactly is THIS?" she shouted. The strange woman jumped in fear.

"Darling," the woman asked, "who is this woman?" Before he could answer, Granny granted Gene his original request by throwing her wedding ring at his face.

"I WAS Mrs. McCauley," she retorted, "but now, you're it!" And with that, she bolted down the street to the courthouse.

"What do I have to do to get a divorce?" Sandy proclaimed as she stormed through the door of the circuit court clerk. Cedar Rapids was still a small town, and no introductions were necessary - not that she was in the mood to entertain formalities.

"Oh Sandy, you can't divorce Gene if he has orders to deploy. You have to wait for him to come back stateside." The fact that Gene's lies had permeated all the way to the courthouse only infuriated her more.

"The son of a bitch is just down the street with his pregnant whore. Give me that paperwork before he does leave this time!"

The clerk was shaken. "Um, OK, but I have just a few questions to ask you. First, what grounds are you filing on?"

"Adultery," Sandy flatly announced.

"Great. And what address should we send the papers to?"

Sandy gave the clerk the address to the only friend she suspected would be in on Gene's lies.

"And one final question - are you currently pregnant?"

Sandy sat down and was quiet for the first time since arriving. "Why does that matter?" she asked.

"Well," the clerk explained, "if you're currently pregnant, the judge will deny the divorce, and you'll have to come back after you have the baby. It's state law."

"Then, no," Sandy answered, "I am not pregnant."

And with that, the papers were drawn and delivered.

The 1950s were not a time for a pregnant mother to be single, but my Granny stood firm in her resolve to make the best life that she could for her boys. So she moved back in with her mother and found work - and Jack found her there.

"I told you, he's a no-good squid," Jack teased her. "When are you gonna go out with me?"

Sandy snapped back at him, "What kind of disgusting man would want a pregnant mother of three?"

Jack got serious. "The kind of man who knows the value of a good woman with three boys and actually wants to raise a family." And just 11 days after giving birth to her fourth child, Sandy married Jack. She would give him two more children, and he would give her boys his last name. Jack Wells was the only grandfather I ever knew, and my dad made it clear that Jack was the only man who deserved that title.

I heard a story at my Grandpa Jack's funeral that he had run into Gene not long after the confrontation on the street. I was told that Jack confronted Gene, telling him to stay away from my grandmother, father, and uncles, promising that he would win Granny's heart and take care of the family that Gene left behind. I don't know if that's true, but I know that Gene only came back once, years later, asking my Granny for money. She made the entire event uncomfortable for him, making him pose for photos with each boy to have a picture of the man they may ask about one day. She knew he wouldn't be back. I have the photograph of Gene with my father, and the discomfort in both of them permeates throughout the picture.

Winding through the rich timber forests of Raymondville, Missouri, is Big Creek, a shallow tributary of the Current River. The creek is bordered by cliffs that have become popular for their numerous caves. I once read a story told from the point of view of a young man who enjoyed riding his horse along Big Creek and stopped one day in a lush field to watch a young girl gathering buckets of water from the creek. His account describes her as maybe 7 or 8 years old, small but seemingly strong. He watched the girl load the buckets onto a tree branch, hoist the branch onto her tiny shoulders, and begin climbing a trail up a bluff that overlooked the creek. Much to his surprise, the young girl easily climbed to almost the top of the bluff and disappeared into one of the many caves. In his story, he speculates that the cave was a hiding place for her to play. He remembers that the cave had been nicknamed Morgan Cave, and Anna O'Brien's 1939 dissertation titled "Place

Names of Five Central Counties of Missouri" verifies that the name was given after the family who lived in the cave. Anna O'Brien was correct - my great-grandparents raised their family in this cave during the Great Depression until the death of my great-grandfather. It is only by coincidence that Grandpa Wells would buy the land that included the same lush field described in this account, and my father and uncles would ride horses to this cave and explore the remains of the food, furniture, and household items left behind by the family that would one day become his in-laws.

Minerva Morgan Labbee was quite the opposite of Sandy Wells. Where Sandy was brash and bold, Minerva - or, as we affectionately called her, Grandma Nervie - was small and quiet. She stood just a few inches under five feet tall, and I am told that the only time she weighed over 100 pounds was during any of her ten pregnancies. What she lacked in stature, my grandmother made up for in heart.

One blessing of my chaotic upbringing was that I had the gift of spending a year of my early childhood living with my Grandma Nervie. When the house was empty from people hurrying off to work and school, I would plant myself at Grandma's feet and beg to hear another story. She told of growing up poor in rural Missouri, meeting my grandfather, and listening to his band play on the radio each week. She told me stories of raising her children and how devastated she was to lose two of them in infancy. My grandfather had died two years before I was born, but Grandma filled me with enough stories that I felt like I knew this gentle giant of a man.

I don't remember hearing from Grandma Nervie a single complaint about anything. She painted for me the picture of her walking up a steep hill, carrying buckets of water on each of her sides, but she left out the part about her living in a cave. Grandma talked about how sad she was the night that her father died but never described to me the details of how the townsfolk had to ride donkeys along the bluff to carry him out of the cave on a cold winter's night. These were all details that I would put together as an adult, hearing accounts from the people of Raymondville and reading local folklore. When I would ask Grandma why we were poor, she would correct me and say, "we don't have things, but we aren't poor. We have more love in this family than most families, and we have God." And she never had less than a smile when she corrected me on that fact.

My mother was almost jealous of my connection with her mother. Our bond became the most apparent one summer night when I was seven years old. We moved to Colorado, building our mountain home around us as we lived in an old, shabby trailer. I had come down with a stomach bug the day before, and since I had no bedroom, I was wrapped in blankets with cool towels on my head in the living room as my parents entertained their close friends, Linda and Bo.

As they were leaving, Linda came to me to give me a gentle kiss on the forehead and said, "you poor dear - you'll be better soon."

"But I won't," I blurted out in a moment of lucidity, "because my grandma just died."

My superstitious mother jumped to her feet. She screamed at me. "Why the hell did you say that? Debra Kay, don't say stuff like that!"

My grandmother had been recently moved from a hospital to a nursing home, much against the wishes of all of her children. Still, she was only in her late 50s, and after a series of strokes, the doctors insisted on sending her somewhere that could care for her on a full-time basis. My mother, child number nine of a family of ten, felt strongly that this was a betrayal to her mom. And it had become obvious that I had just betrayed her as well.

"Why in the world would you just SAY that?" she went on.

Linda was quick to come to my defense. "Dottie, she's running a fever," she said. "She's been throwing up for two days and is probably dehydrated. Be easy on the child." And, after calming my mother down and settling me back down to sleep, Linda and Bo left.

I don't know exactly how much time had gone by, but I heard my stepdad announce that a car was coming up the driveway. He assumed it was Linda and Bo, and began searching the living room for what they may have forgotten. Mom answered the door to find her sister - my Aunt Linda - standing there in tears, being braced by my Uncle David. We had no telephone nor even electricity, so my aunt and uncle would often have to make the drive from their home when there was news from the family.

"Mama died!" my Aunt Linda blurted out. My mother didn't miss a beat.

"WHAT DID YOU DO??" she hissed at me. My stepdad had to grab her and physically force her to sit down. I started crying uncontrollably as he explained to our family my momentary outburst. "How did you KNOW?"

I couldn't stop crying. "I don't know, Mom," I stuttered defensively. "I just saw her in my head and she said 'goodbye' and she was so happy to finally be with Grandpa." Nothing about seeing my grandmother seemed unusual to me at the time, but now I felt insecure about the entire ordeal.

Raymondville, Missouri, is a small village in southern Missouri with a rich logging history. The Missouri Ozarks experienced a great timber boom between 1880 and 1910, and hence, the small village that still retains the nickname "Timbertown" was born. Long after the 6 million acres of Missouri forest was cut and stripped, Raymondville continued to serve sawmills and loggers. It was the quiet farm life that drew my Grandpa Wells to relocate his family and buy a sawmill, and it was the timber money that brought my Grandpa Labbee's family there.

The contrast between the Wells and Labbee families was stark. The Wells family was known for their drive to succeed, but sometimes, that focus came across as intimidating. My Labbee grandparents, however, were among the poorest families in town, and yet, they were notoriously generous. Many people have told me stories about the days when my Grandpa Labbee drove a propane gas truck and would short some deliveries by just a few gallons until he had enough to make a trip to a family who couldn't afford to put propane in their tanks. He would calculate just enough to get them through the upcoming winter storm. Those stories never set well with me, as it was essentially stealing, but my grandfather thought it was more important that the sick and elderly stay warm than someone with means paying an extra dollar or two for a propane delivery.

The term "poverty" encompasses many types of lifestyles that, by economic definition, exist below some government threshold of income and/or asset accumulation. Relative poverty refers to those households who live below a specific median income, but who still are able to afford the basic needs of life (housing, food, and clothing, for example). I can remember seeing those families and wishing that I had all that they did. When I speak of my childhood in poverty, I am telling of an experience of abject poverty - deep poverty that spans back more generations than I can count.

I have a memory of being in sixth grade, living in a new town, and attending a new school. A very pretty girl in my class was whispering to her friend as they watched me stand and walk to the pencil sharpener. I stared sharply at the girls, making them fully aware that I knew that their conversation was about me. Finally, one of the girls stood up and walked to me.

"Is that the only pair of jeans you own?" she asked with a smirk.

"Yes," I replied dryly, "it is. And these are my only shoes." I pointed to the canvas threads on my feet, which were tattered with holes in the toes and along the sides. "Is there anything else you want to ask me?"

She was only momentarily humbled before snapping back "oh really? Is that why you always wear the same shirts, too?" She looked at her friend and they had a laugh.

"It is." I remained determined to make her understand exactly what she was pointing out. "I have three shirts. I have to wash them in the bathroom sink because we can't afford to buy a washing machine. My mom doesn't have a job, and I live in the housing projects." I glared at her friend. "Is there anything else about me you want to poke fun at while you're here?"

It was apparent to me that she didn't expect that I would actually own up to her accusations.

"Um, no," she said. She looked at her friend, who motioned for her to sit down. "I'm sorry. I just thought you didn't care about what you wear." I saw a sting in her eye and realized that she, too, knew poverty. Most of us in that town did. I had hit a nerve with her. She never spoke to or about me again.

That was the reality of the poverty I knew. For me, school lunch was often my favorite meal of the day. My mother didn't *not* feed me, but she didn't have much to feed me and during the years that it was just the two of us, there was no actual dinner time. I can't actually remember eating too many meals at home during those years, as I was very aware that any food in the refrigerator or cabinets would need to feed me over the weekend when I didn't have a school meal. We lived a lot on commodity foods from the government food pantry - mostly rice, pinto beans, and processed cheese. The processed cheese was very popular in our neighborhood, and Mom would often sell the block of cheese for cash to buy cigarettes, leaving just rice and beans for the month.

My father's family lived in more of the relative poverty realm. My grandfather was able to purchase a few hundred acres with some livestock and build a house in Raymondville for his wife and six children. Money was tight, but the family was resourceful enough to learn how to run a sawmill for steady income, and the children learned how to work horses and cattle with manual tools.

When he was only fifteen, my father sat his parents down and explained to them how much more efficient the farm would operate, if they would invest in a tractor. My grandfather wouldn't hear of it. They didn't have the cash for a tractor, and he didn't want to carry an extra loan for something that may not even work. But my father wouldn't give up. He ran numbers and drew out a plan, and when my grandfather wouldn't hear any more of it, my father had his mother drive him to the bank so that they could hear his plan. It worked. The banker secured a loan to my father - with his mother cosigning - and bought a tractor. As livid as my grandfather was, he couldn't argue when less than a year had passed and my father had used the extra income from the work he did with the tractor to pay the loan in full.

And that was the biggest difference between my two families. My mother's family had always accepted that we were poor, that poverty was just our burden to bear. My father's family, however, saw poverty as just an obstacle, and my father was determined to overcome it.

On January 27, 1973, the United States government announced an end to conscription, or what was commonly known as "the draft". From then until 1980, the US had no selective service system in place and depended fully upon volunteers to fill over 800,000 security jobs throughout the armed forces. The low pay and grueling duty requirements made these positions distasteful for the college-educated and entrepreneurial youth, but the opportunity to leave small-town America and get paid to receive on-the-job training was a dream to many young men and women whose families could not otherwise afford the luxury of higher education. As such, the 1970s and early 1980s saw a huge influx of poor young people volunteering for military service - a phenomenon commonly referred to as the "poverty draft".

It was never Dennis Wells's dream to join the US Air Force. He was a highly motivated young man who excelled at math and science, even warranting his teachers to create special physics and calculus curriculum for him in high school. Dennis very much loved farm life, and he had a gift for working with horses. In his early teens, he heard a calling for training horses and found his skills to be in demand throughout the county. Dennis set his sights on veterinary medicine and was accepted to the University of Missouri pre-veterinary program on scholarship.

For everything Dennis was, Dorothy Labbee was equal and opposite. Dorothy was a small brunette with a curvaceous figure and a flair for life. She was the ninth of ten Labbee children, though she often competed with her youngest sister for the attention normally fawned toward the baby of the family.

At some point in her early adult years, her friends nicknamed her Dottie, and she loved the new moniker and all of the sass that came with it.

Dottie struggled with school and reading, and would later learn that she suffered from a debilitating case of dyslexia that forced her to drop out of high school during her freshman year. She had no issues with attracting boys, though, and she decided at an early age to capitalize upon this.

I never learned how or why my parents met, though I imagine that it wasn't hard to run into one another in a town as small as Raymondville. I do know that my father was not my mother's only suitor, and I'm not even sure that he was her favorite. I'm sure that both of them were just as shocked as their families when, at the beginning of the summer of 1976, they learned that Dottie was pregnant.

Raymondville is the kind of town that has no secrets - and I have reason to suspect that my conception became the loudest whisper of the summer of 1976. My Grandpa Labbee had died the year before from injuries he had sustained in a logging accident. I've heard that my mother's wild streak was unstoppable after his death, and I was the result of that.

"She had a lot of boyfriends," my Granny Wells would remind me as an adult. "I kept telling Dennis to just let her go, but he had to save her. Hell, you could be anyone's daughter, but no," she would tartly express, "my Dennis was a good boy and wasn't going to see any kid go without a dad."

Granny was wrong - if my eyes and sharp face didn't give me away, my awkward intellect should have. She wasn't alive to see that AncestryDNA would prove her theory wrong, but she was always the only person who doubted my paternity. I was born on a cold January day in 1977 and was identical to my father from my first breath.

I've heard the stories of the drama between Dennis and

Dottie - how he dropped out of college to work at the local sporting goods factory, but she didn't slow down for a minute to stay at home with me. I've heard that they lied to her mother about getting married, but enough dramatic fights in the town square would send the truth rushing back home to Grandma Nervie. And finally, I heard that my dad wanted to break up for good in the autumn of 1977, but an attorney friend of the family reminded him that he had no rights to see me without a custodial agreement - and the easiest way to get one was to marry and divorce my mother.

I don't believe that my father married my mother with the intention of divorce. I think that, for a brief moment, he fantasized that they could actually be a family if they made the right decisions. I know that my mother believed that marriage would put an end to her poverty, especially with my dad's plan to join the US Air Force. And so, my parents were married on October 31, 1977, and my father was on a bus to Lackland Air Force Base on November 1.

My dad, being Dennis, couldn't even half-ass the military enough to just get by. His test scores immediately flagged him as a top recruit, and soon he found himself in school to become an Arab linguist. Mom was so excited when she learned that linguistic school was in Monterey, California, and even more giddy when the orders came to send our family to Crete, Greece. Mom had won the poverty lottery.

I have very few memories of my parents' marriage. I can remember waking up to my dad carrying me into the living room, where we would camp on the floor with a lot of thick blankets and a tray of cheese and olives. I loved those mornings. I learned later that he was training overnight, and my wake-up was his start to unwinding. My mother was a young and beautiful 21-year-old woman who loved the social aspects to living on a Greek island. She would spend her afternoons and evenings at local restaurants and clubs, timing her return home to the time that my father would need to report to duty, sleeping off her excursions over the majority of the next day while my dad caught intermittent naps with me.

One oddly vivid memory that I have of our time in Greece is of nights spent with a woman whom I called "Aunt Nora". I don't recall the relationship that she had with my parents, but I do remember that she would babysit me when neither was home to put me to bed. I loved Nora. Nora was the daughter of a Palestinian refugee with dark, curly hair, and her mother's history gave her an advantage as an Arab linguist. I loved how she spoke to me in real talk, not baby talk. I loved her warm smile and even her big glasses. Even as a toddler, I got the sense that Nora was a smart and confident woman, and I wanted to be just like her.

Nora gifted me a stuffed Yeti-style toy, with hair from his head to his ankles. On the bottom of one of his bare feet was written "Love, Aunt Nora." I would ask repeatedly "what does this say?" and people around me would read it out loud. After a while, I knew what it said, I just loved hearing those words.

I have another vivid memory of being on a plane with my mom, holding this stuffed Yeti, and looking out the window at a vast blue ocean. I was so excited to be on a plane with my mom - mostly just having this rare alone time with my mother. I put the stuffed animal up to the window and saw that writing on the foot. I asked my mother "Mommy, what does this say?" Instead of answering me, she burst into tears.

The next year, Nora and my father welcomed their first child, and "Aunt Nora" became "Mommy Nora."

THE CADET YEARS

Leaving Greece meant that my mother had to learn how to become an adult. She had only completed the eighth grade, she had not yet learned how to drive, and her brief period in Job Corps abruptly ended when she was expelled for sneaking off-campus. She had no skills and even less education, and by the time we came back to the US, my Grandma Nervie's health had begun to fail, forcing her to move in with my Aunt Louise and leaving Mom with no parent to fall back on.

The first year was stark for us, and that is where I found my light.

Mom chose first to try her luck in Raymondville, even though she only had a brother left there. She got a job at the local shoe factory and caught rides to work with my Aunt Shirley. I stayed with a babysitter, Mrs. Barton. I loved days with Mrs. Barton and the other children that she watched. She made us nice sandwiches with fruit on the side and let us watch the popular TV show "Dallas" with her on the noon syndication. We kept repeating "JR's dead!" as we ran around the house, stopping only to pretend for a moment that we were wearing some of the pretty dresses that we saw on the show. I was only three years old, but I already knew that I loved pretty dresses.

Mrs. Barton lived close to us, and one evening, she came by to help me put on a pretty dress in preparation for my first church visit. I was excited because she made such a big deal of it, and I am guessing that it was during Easter because I remember spending the first part of the night dying eggs and making crafts out of pipe cleaners and egg cartons. I loved the crafting so much that I asked to stay to help clean up while services started upstairs.

Once the basement classroom was clean, I marched my way upstairs to look for Mrs. Barton. I didn't get very far through the door of the church before a man in the front, standing at a wooden pulpit and speaking into a microphone, pointed in my direction and said loudly "There! Look at that poor child!"

I looked around for the poor child he was talking about but saw no one else.

"She did not choose to be here, but here she is, paying for the sins of her parents."

I felt bad for the girl he was talking about. I didn't know what a sin was, but his voice didn't make it sound nice.

"And now here she is, paying for the lust and fornication that they gave themselves to; God tells us that she will carry the sins of her parents, and so will the generations after her."

He was screaming and it was scaring me. I started crying.

"See? She knows she's the result of sin – look at the tears coming down her face! She knows that hell is waiting for people who don't repent!"

Wait. I knew what hell was – it was that place that my mother told people she didn't like to go to when they made her mad. I didn't want to go to hell! I didn't want to pay for whatever those things were that he said my mom and dad did, and I didn't know how to get out of it. He kept going on, but I was crying too hard to hear him. The entire church was watching me with their hands raised shouting "Amen!" but no one was coming to console me.

Then, a louder voice came over me. "Calm down, child," the soothing voice said. "He is wrong. All children belong to Me."

I stopped crying. I looked up but didn't see anyone.

"You are mine."

I peed.

Suddenly, Mrs. Barton broke through a crowd of hand-raising, "amen" chanting people and swooped me up. "Oh no!" she exclaimed. "Your pretty new shoes!" And she got me out of there and took me home.

When we got home, Mrs. Barton was a mixture of concerned, frustrated, and embarrassed. "It didn't go well," she told my mother. "She got to the sermon and wet herself, so we had to come home."

Mrs. Barton left, and I found myself frustrated that she didn't tell the entire story.

"What happened?" my mother asked me.

"That preacher man told me I'm going to hell," I said. Mom got furious.

"He told you what?" she shouted.

"He said you and Daddy sinned and I'm going to hell."

Mom got angrier. "That's why I didn't want to come back to this God-forsaken town! These people never mind their own business and I'll be damned if they start treating my daughter like a bastard!"

"But wait, Mom," I said, now calming her down. "Jesus told me that it's not true."

"Did Mrs. Barton tell you that?" she asked.

"No," I insisted, "Jesus did. He said that all children belong to him. So I'm not scared anymore."

She was so confused.

"He yelled over the preacher and told me I'm his!" Then I asked, "Who is Jesus?" And that night, my mother pulled out a children's bible that she had been holding for me and read me the story of the nativity. To her credit, she never questioned nor disputed anything I told her that night. For years after that, we'd remember that conversation with joy and laugh about the night that Jesus claimed me and made me pee myself.

Not long after the Easter incident, Mom decided that she wanted to be closer to her mom, and we moved to Cadet, Missouri. Mom had been born in Washington County and spent most of her school years there, so for her, we were home. She also never liked to be far from her mother or any of her sisters, and I don't think that my uncle in Raymondville gave her the same sense of comfort that she needed. She still couldn't drive, so keeping a viable job became an obstacle for her. By now, the divorce had settled, and Mom was earning a whopping $160 each month in child support – guaranteed since Dad was in the military and all garnishments were paid directly from his government check.

Mom found a small camper trailer in a part of Washington County known as Hopewell, though I still haven't found anything well or even hopeful about it. We lived in a trailer park community called Green Acres, just like the TV show but without a glamorous matriarch or pet pig. We couldn't afford a TV, so Mom played the radio all day, and that was when I discovered that I could sing like Dolly Parton – or so the old men told me. My mom had a beautiful singing voice, and she paid attention to the instruction that her musician father taught her as a girl. We bonded over music, with Mom correcting my flat notes and encouraging me to take risks with my voice. I learned to yodel to "Jolene", and practiced my octaves to "I'll Always Love You", right in the road for everyone to see, with my mother beaming from the doorway. Then and today, I recoil when strangers try to talk to me, but I have no fear of breaking out in song for everyone on the street to hear.

Mom's rebellious nature failed to be tamed by motherhood and marriage. She soon made friends with Jane, a tall, slender blonde woman with two children and a husband in a biker gang. Jane had a deep voice and a strong presence. My mother was only 5'1" and sometimes could put on enough weight to weigh 100 pounds, and I know that Jane made her feel safe and gave her the courage to stand up for herself.

I only saw Jane's husband once, when he pulled into the driveway on a loud motorcycle with two other motorcycles behind him. The entire house shook with fear as he came inside to address Jane. I had never seen Jane back down to anyone, but she was quiet and meek when he addressed her. They conversed, then he nodded his head at his children, pointed a finger, and said "y'all be good for your mama", and left. The bikes were so loud, and the men looked so mean. It took several minutes for anyone to speak again and for me to get the courage to ask the children why they were so scared of their dad.

"Because he's a Hell's Angel", the boy said.

"I didn't know that hell had angels," I replied. "I thought only heaven had angels."

The girl giggled. "No, silly," she said. "He's a biker. A bad guy. He hurts people if they don't do what you want them to do."

I thought about my own dad. "But he wouldn't hurt you or your mom," I said confidently.

The boy got quiet. "He hurts my mom a lot," he said. "We aren't supposed to be living here. He told her that he would kill her if she moved out, but she did and he found us."

"So why didn't he kill her?"

"Because she has to do stuff for him," the little girl replied. "Bad stuff. That's the only way he lets her stay here."

"But he doesn't hurt you, does he?" I asked.

They both got quiet. "He has," the boy said. "And he hurt our sister. That's why she doesn't live with us anymore. He hurt her a lot."

"Mom said she'd rather die than have him hurt us again," the little girl said. "So she does the bad stuff to keep him away."

Jane's husband was soon sent to prison, and the house lit up like a party. That still wasn't enough to teach Jane and Mom to stay away from bad boys. I have memories of being dragged to parties at the nearby lake, with drunken men falling over us kids and our mothers smoking pot and flirting their way through the crowd. It was so normal for us, but terrifying to look back upon.

One night, the bad boy drama found its way to our trailer. My mom was cooking dinner on our tiny gas stove, which was directly in front of the trailer door. I was sitting in the chair next to the stove in the nearby sitting area when a man burst through the door wielding a knife. We both screamed, and the man grabbed my mother to pull her to him. I remember seeing her long, chestnut hair fly into the flames, and I did the only thing I could think to do – I pushed my way between my mother and the stove and turned off the burner before she lit into a ball of fire. My mother acted quickly and took the opportunity to grab my arm and throw me out of the front door. Instinctually, I started to run back to her when she yelled "Sissy, RUN! Just RUN!"

I did. I ran but didn't know where to go. Jane and her children had just moved, so I couldn't go to her trailer. I didn't trust the landlord's son because he had scared me many times as I played along the road. So I ran to the left as if I was running to the highway until the man holding a knife to my mother's throat stopped watching me. As soon as he closed the door, I darted back behind the trailers that were across the street and knocked on the back door of a couple that I knew were nice.

"Debra?" the woman asked, "where is Dottie?"

"There...is a...man," I was out of breath. The woman called to her husband to come quick, and I worked to catch my breath.

"A man with a knife and he tried to burn Mommy's hair!" The nice man quickly shot out the front door while yelling "call the police!" back to his wife.

I wanted to go home. She told me that I needed to stay with her and her children until her husband came back. It was dark before he did.

"Debra," he said, "you're staying with us tonight. You can sleep with the girls."

"But my mommy!" I protested, "I want to be with my mommy!"

With that, a man in a uniform with a gun on his belt came into the house and asked me for my name. "My name is Debra Kay Wells and I'm not supposed to talk to strangers."

The man kneeled down and smiled. "Well," he said, "I'm not a stranger. I'm a police officer. I need you to tell me what happened tonight." I knew police officers from TV – I watched "CHiPS" and his uniform looked a lot like theirs, so I decided to trust him.

After telling him what had happened, the police officer put his hand on my shoulder. "You're a very smart and brave little girl," he said. "You saved your mom's life."

"Can I go home now?" I asked.

"Not tonight," he said. "Your mom is ok, but she has to go to the hospital for the night to be safe. She said you can stay here until she comes home."

The next morning, my Aunt Louise brought my mother home. Mom packed my backpack and sent me off to stay with Aunt Louise and Grandma Nervie. I couldn't have been more excited.

Aunt Louise and Uncle Teet had two children of their own: Joyce, who was 15 years older than me and, since she was so close in age to my mother and only a year younger than Aunt Brenda, was really the honorary baby of Mom's siblings; and Keith, a rough and tumble boy 10 years older than me, but who I loved like he was my own brother. Joyce was tall and blonde with Farrah Fawcett-style hair and brown eyes. I remember thinking that she was a miracle because I was always told that blonde people only had blue eyes, like me. Joyce was smart and funny and was the best tennis player in town.

Keith was the rebel child. He had a charming smile and his mom said he could con a con artist out of a job. I loved him. Keith would carry me around on his back and let me wear his favorite t-shirts to bed. I didn't like when his girlfriends would visit because he would try to show off for them and act macho. I didn't like Macho Keith, I liked my teddy bear pseudo big brother.

It was apparent that Keith got his soft spot for little girls from his dad. My Uncle Teet was wrapped around my finger from the first time I crawled up on his lap. He was a quiet man who my mother described to look like John Wayne, but sing like Johnny Cash. He would rise at 4 AM, make a pot of coffee, and sit at the kitchen table with his old guitar. Everyone knew that if they got up early enough, they'd get a front-row seat to the Morning Teet Show. By now, I had learned that I could sing, and Uncle Teet would harmonize with me. I loved that. I made him teach me how to do it. Soon, it was the Morning Teet and Debra Show, with Aunt Louise and Grandma Nervie shouting "Encore! Encore!" from the living room.

After everyone would go to work and school, I'd have a day alone with my grandmother. That was probably my favorite part of the day. That was when we would have our long talks about her own childhood, and when she'd tell me stories of my grandfather and reassure me that he would have loved me just as much as she did. We would watch TV together – our favorite show was "Captain Kangaroo" – and Grandma would teach me how to make basic crochet stitches.

I confided in Grandma that Jesus had visited me. She nodded. "I gave you to Him," she said matter-of-factly, "I'm not surprised that He talked to you. I've prayed over you every day of your life." She looked down at me with a smile. "I'm glad you know Him now."

I spent the next Easter with Grandma, dressing up in our best dresses and taking photos in the front yard. Some of the photos from that day are still my favorites. Grandma explained to me that we were celebrating Jesus and that the eggs were a symbol of the new life that He gave to us. It was confusing, but I can understand why a 4-year-old didn't need the entire story yet. I had no idea that Easter was for Jesus! So was Christmas, she told me. It was a whole new world opening up to me! Grandma shared photos of a woman she called Mary and told me that she was Jesus's mom. My grandmother was raised Lutheran but had a solid devotion to the Virgin Mary that I wouldn't understand for decades to come. This was all knowledge that I absorbed as fast as I could. I felt like my grandmother had opened an entirely new world to me, and I was excited about it.

Soon, Mom came back to get me. She had a new man with

her, and my grandmother seemed to know him well. He had dark, curly hair, and the most piercing blue eyes that I had ever seen. Grandma jumped up to hug his neck when he came into the house, which made me immediately feel comfortable with him. Mom introduced him as David and announced that they would be getting married soon. They wanted me to move to Independence with them after the wedding, which would be held at Hopewell Church. My grandmother was elated.

Grandmother knew David so well because he was the son of her sister-in-law, and, consequently, her nephew. David and his brothers were adults when June married my great-uncle, so Mom didn't know him as a cousin. Grandma knew him well because she had spent several months with her brother after he remarried, and became very close to David and his brothers. I still don't know what brought him and my mother together from across the state, but I know not to underestimate the power of my mother's ability to land a man.

David and my mother were married in the spring of 1981, and we moved with him back to his home in Independence. I adored David and called him "Daddy David" at home. I didn't get much time to settle in with the family before my other family came calling me back to my other home.

My dad and Nora welcomed my brother Josh around the same time that my mother was celebrating her second wedding. It was an exciting time overall for me. After the wedding, my dad came to take me off the hands of the newlyweds and brought me to Maryland, to live in base with him, Nora, and Josh. I loved being a big sister, though Josh was a pretty independent baby and didn't take to anyone other than his mother fussing over him.

My memories of life in Maryland are happy and idyllic.

Nora had left her career in the US Air Force to stay at home with me and Josh while Dad trained for sometimes days at a time. We lived on base in a two-story townhome, and our front door faced the local playground. I wasn't old enough to attend school yet, and I was so jealous of the girls on the playground who were.

Very few of my playmates looked like me. In fact, I can't remember having any friends with my pale complexion and bright yellow hair. Most of the girls that I saw had dark skin and thick curly hair that they wore in tight braids with bright barrettes or colored beads. I wanted braids, too. I was jealous of the many fun accessories that jingled when my friends shook their heads. I would ask Nora to put my hair in barrettes, too, but they always seemed to fall out of my thin hair as soon as I stepped outside.

I finally approached Nora with my idea.

"I want braids," I told her one morning.

She started to part my hair down the middle when I stopped her. "Not like that," said. "Little braids, like her." I pointed out the dining room window to one of my friends.

Nora laughed lightly. "No, sweetheart," she said, "your hair is too fine for that. Your head will burn if we do that."

"But I want it," I said determinedly. "I won't let my head burn, I promise." Still, Nora stood firm in her answer, and I had to face my friends with only two side braids down my blonde head.

I decided to take matters into my own hands. If Mommy Nora wasn't going to make me as pretty as the other girls, I'd recruit one of them to do it.

I asked one of the older girls on the playground to braid my hair to look like hers. She laughed the same way that Nora had laughed at me. "You can't, silly," she said. "You're white. White girls can't wear cornrows" And then she left to meet the school bus that had just pulled up to the playground.

I was confused about what she saw on me that was white. My hair was bright, but it was really more yellow than white. If she was wrong about my hair color, she must have also been wrong about the braids. Her younger sister, who sported the same tiny braids that the older girl was wearing, came up to offer her services instead.

"I can braid your hair," she said. "I see my mom do it all the time. I'll go get my barrettes." And with that, my goal was coming to fruition.

The little girl and I spent several painful hours after lunch behind the central air units with her pulling at my scalp and me howling in pain. "It has to be tight so it doesn't fall out," she said. I was in tears. I could barely have my hair brushed without crying, and this felt like torture. But in the end, it was all worth the effort as I sported just over a dozen tiny braids down my head and to my back. I spent the afternoon playing with my friends and feeling like I finally fit in with the other girls.

Just before the school bus came back to return the older kids, Nora called me back into the house. She shrieked in horror. "What did you do?" she yelled, "Your scalp is red as a beet!"

I didn't want to tell her how bad my scalp hurt. I was too proud to admit that she was right. Instead, I sat in a dining room chair for over an hour while Nora drenched my scalp in cream and proceeded to pull the tight rows out of my hair. I cried. She comforted me but stayed firm in reminding me that she was Mom and that came with some experience that I did not yet have.

I told the girls on the playground what had happened. The young girl who had invested her time and talent into my tight braids was devastated that all of her work was so quickly destroyed. Finally, the older girl who had been refusing to touch my hair sat us down behind the large air conditioner unit and schooled us on the differences between us.

"We braid our hair like that because we have black hair and it gets hard to brush," she explained.

"But mine is hard to brush, too," I said, still trying to fit in with my friends. "Doesn't it hurt when you braid it?"

"Sometimes," she said, "But we get used to it." She continued her explanation with "And we don't get sunburned like you do."

"Why?" I asked. It was unfair to me.

"Because black people don't burn like white people."

Wait. I was so confused now, as was my young friend.

"Do you see how dark my skin is?" she asked me. "I'm black."

"But you aren't," I said, "you are brown."

"Maybe, but they call me black. See your skin? You are white."

"I am not!" I protested, "My skin is pink!" I was getting upset. I had learned my colors in Head Start and I knew what I saw.

"I know," she agreed. "But this is what people call us."

"It sounds mean," my young friend protested. "I hear people say it to my mama and they aren't nice."

"I know," the older girl said. "People like to make us different, but we aren't."

"I don't think we are," I announced stubbornly.

"We aren't," she agreed. "If you turn my skin inside-out, it's white on the inside. And if you turn your skin inside-out, it's black on the inside. That's why both of us have red blood when we get a cut." This started to make some sense to me, even though I had never seen the other side of my skin.

Another older girl quickly interjected. "Besides," she

started, "our dads are brothers because they fly together, they fight together, and they save each others' lives. That makes us cousins."

I was confused again. "What are you talking about?"

"They fly planes," the girl explained. "That's why we live here. Our dads are training to fight bad people, and when they are in the air, they are brothers."

The brother concept was completely new to me. I had no idea that my dad flew a plane, even though I had been to the hangar with him and saw his jumpsuit. My four-year-old mind didn't have the capacity to put the information together. I loved the idea of all of these girls being my family, but my dad had a lot of explaining to do.

MY OTHER MOM

It felt like the months with Dad and Nora went by too fast, but soon, it was time for me to return to my mom and her new husband, David. I was pleasantly surprised to see a plump belly on my mother when she met us at the door - I knew from my time with Nora that this meant a new baby. Even though Joshua never seemed interested in playing with me or letting me dote on him, I did enjoy participating in his daily routine with Nora. I knew that this would be a bonding experience for me and Mom.

Mom was excited to share the baby with me, too. While David was at work, Mom would show me photos from the pamphlets that her doctor had provided, so that I could see what the baby looked like during different stages of her pregnancy. I was the first to feel a kick, and I would giggle incessantly while Mom's stomach stretched from the baby turning - and, even as uncomfortable as it was for her, my mother was excited to call me into the room when it would happen.

Expecting a new baby did not slow down my mother and her husband. They kept an active social calendar, which was easy since we lived so close to his family. David's brother or father would sit with me while Mom and David went to friends' houses for barbecues or to watch football games. They were still young - only in their mid-20s - and they wanted to enjoy as much of their time together as they could before the baby arrived.

For the most part, I was happy to stay home watching television with David's family. I liked them, and they would let me eat ice cream and stay up past my bedtime. One night, though, I became agitated at my mother's insistence on leaving. I didn't have a reason, I just didn't want her to go.

That night, David and Mom failed to come home. I remember waking up on the couch and asking if they were home yet and getting a worried response from David's dad, Ralph, that they were still out, and he would be sure to wake me up when they came home. I fell back asleep, only to wake myself up screaming.

"The baby's hurt!" I screeched, before even realizing that I was awake. Ralph rushed to my side.

"No, sweetie," he said calmly, "You just had a bad dream."

"Where is my mommy?" I demanded.

Ralph seemed unsettled. "She and Daddy are still out," he answered. I remember that I didn't like the uneasiness in his voice.

"Help them!" I screamed again. "Mommy and the baby are hurt!"

Now David's brother, Troy, sat next to the couch with Ralph. "Dad," he said calmly, "I think she's picking up that we're nervous. Let's take her to bed." But I refused to go, and no one forced me. Instead, I cried myself to sleep, just as scared about what I was saying as Ralph and Troy seemed to be.

I know that it was the next morning when David and Mom came through the front door because I remember waking up on the same couch and seeing the sun coming through the balcony door.

"Where have you been?" Ralph yelled as soon as he heard the door open. "You told me you'd be home at midnight, and this little girl had nightmares all night!"

David put his hands on Ralph's arms as if to calm him down, while my mother rushed to me in tears and hugged me tightly. "We had an accident," David answered. "We've been in the hospital. Dorothy needs to go to bed."

"Mommy, is the baby ok?" I asked her. She held me closer and started crying.

"We'll be OK," she whispered. Meanwhile, I could hear David continuing with his story.

"...so then, we stopped at the light and this guy just rammed us right from behind. Didn't even stop! I got out and screamed at him 'hey, my wife is 7 months pregnant, what the hell are you doing?' I almost punched him when Dorothy started screaming that she was bleeding!"

The men rushed to Mom's side.

"I'm OK," she said weakly. "The baby is OK, I just have to be on bed rest for the next few months."

"She almost lost my baby!" David exclaimed. "I want to find that son of a bitch and kill him!"

Ralph turned white. "Debie said it!" he yelled, "Debie told me that the baby was hurt!" I felt my face turn red as the entire room turned toward me. My mother just held me tighter.

"They know," she said softly. "She's already close to this baby. Children just know."

My brother, Roy, was born less than two weeks after my 5th birthday. I spent most of my birthday standing at my mother's belly, begging the baby to come that day. I was born on my aunt's 16th birthday, and I had the idea that the three of us would spend the rest of our lives celebrating together over cake. Just as my brother always does, he did what he wanted, and on his own terms.

Mom had asked her doctor if I could be in the delivery room with her, and we both thought that it would happen. We woke up early in the morning to hear Mom screaming in pain, and David rushed Mom to the car to get to the hospital, with Ralph and me to follow. Roy came fast - by the time Ralph got me to the waiting room, I could already hear my mother screaming in pain. I was horrified. Sometimes, her wails sent me into tears. David made the decision that I would fare better in the waiting room - and I agreed.

I will never forget how happy David was when he ran down the hallway to announce that Mom had given him a son. My brother was born with the brightest blue eyes, and a widow's peak on his hairline to match his father's. The men were proud. I was a little disappointed to hear that I had yet another brother, but I was hopeful that Roy would be more receptive to my attention than Josh had been. I got my wish.

Shortly after Roy's birth, I felt a shift in our small apartment. David had gone from being the doting and affectionate husband that I knew to becoming more abrasive to my mother. My mother was changing, too. She began withdrawing more and becoming more easily agitated. I found myself focusing my attention on my new infant brother, whom I could easily make laugh and coo at my silly antics.

One night, long after my bedtime, I witnessed the change that I felt. I woke up to hearing thuds and yelling from my parent's bedroom. I rushed to the door, only to see David standing over my mother with her dark hair wrapped around his hand, and her head repeatedly hitting the frame of their bed. Her screeching seemed to have no impact on him, just as my tears and Roy's cries didn't. At my mother's command, I slammed the door shut and ran onto the couch. I turned the television volume up as high as I could get it to drown out what I heard from the bedroom and cried myself back to sleep.

In my next memory, David was driving with me, my mother, and Troy when my parents began arguing over the radio station. David pulled into a parking lot and turned around to the back seat, where I sat with his grown brother.

"Hey Troy," he said, cutting off their arguing. "Did you know Dorothy sees a shrink?" My mother let out a horrified squeal.

"David, get back on the road and let it go," Troy replied. But he didn't.

"No, seriously - she's crazy!" David continued with a laugh. "The woman is on all sorts of pills, more shit than me and you do on a Friday night. Tell him, Dorothy!"

My mom burst into tears. She opened the car door when David pulled her arm to get her back into the car. "Come on, honey," he coaxed her, "I'm only kidding."

My mother yelled back at him, throwing her fists at his hands and bursting into tears. Troy finally got out of the back seat to follow her from the car.

While they were outside, I asked David what a shrink is.

"A head doctor," he replied jovially. "Crazy people see them and give them pills to pop."

"Is Mommy crazy?"

David laughed. "You bet your ass she is," he said. I felt sad and overwhelmed by this news.

"Is that why you hit her?" I asked.

David didn't seem alarmed at this question. "Nah," he said casually, "I hit her because she can't shut her mouth." He turned and looked at me seriously. "You gotta learn what a woman's place is, you hear? You keep the house clean, keep the food on the table, and keep your mouth shut. Your mama has a smart mouth and can't keep a thought to herself."

With that, Troy and Mom returned to the car. Mom apologized to David for whatever had started the fight, and we were back on the road. I fought back tears. I couldn't believe what this man that I loved as a father had just said to me.

It took several more physical altercations and arguments over my mother's sanity and David's drug and alcohol use before my mother finally had enough. One morning, my Aunt Louise and Uncle Teet knocked on the door, meeting a relieved Dorothy. I was ordered to grab some bags from my room that my mother had packed for me and Roy, and we were back on our way to Cadet.

I was looking forward to being back at my aunt's house, so it was disappointing to me when my mother immediately found a small trailer to rent for us in Mineral Point. With the new home came newfound freedom for my mother. Our home was sparsely furnished, and we had to hang old beach towels and sheets over the windows for curtains, but it was always full of people. For as much as my mother argued with David over his weekend pot-filled parties, her new life hadn't changed much.

Our trailer was small, and even though I had my own bedroom, I preferred to sleep with my mother. Roy slept in a small add-on to the trailer that doubled as my mother's sewing room, and on the nights when the house was full of people, I would sleep under his crib. I remember that he was teething around this stage, and I spent a lot of nights soothing his cries and letting him bite my fingers for temporary relief from his pain.

I started to feel a shift in our family dynamic. Even though

I was only five, I began to understand the division - it was me and Roy on one side, and my mother on the other. I became Roy's caregiver. He seemed to struggle with crawling and weighed too much for me to carry, so I would roll him around to where I needed him to be. We depended on WIC for our food, and I began to learn how to make a loaf of bread and a block of cheese last as long as possible so that we didn't run out too soon. Mom mostly subsisted on cigarettes and coffee.

Jane was back in our lives, and with her came her brother, who I'll call Allen. I was grateful to have children my age around again. I was also learning how to appreciate my brother's nap times and would fill the silence alone in my room with books that someone had given me. I began to take advantage of the adults that would come through our home, grabbing ones that I trusted and making them read to me. I was so curious to understand what reading was about, and began to memorize the same two books. Soon, I was able to predict what the words on the page were saying, and I moved on to a third book. I now made the adults listen to me try to guess the words on the pages, and when I guessed wrong, I made them explain to me how that word worked. I was teaching myself to read.

At first, Allen entertained this curiosity of mine. He seemed amused that a child could want to learn anything - he came from a world where school was loathed and everyone dropped out as soon as they were legally able to do so. I was different. I watched older kids get onto school buses in the morning and longed for the day when it would be my turn.

Soon, Allen lost patience with everything about me. I overheard him referring to me as "creepy", and he would ostracize me for spending too much time reading and not enough time playing. He was impatient with Roy, too. Roy was 8 months old and still couldn't crawl. He was a happy baby, but he could only roll himself from room to room. My aunts began to notice that something seemed off about his legs, but Allen had convinced Mom that Roy was just a lazy baby. Restrictions began to come down on me, limiting how much I could do for Roy and almost punishing him for being unable to care for himself.

With Allen came a rowdier bunch of friends than Mom had originally attracted. I was scared of many of them, mostly because they had a habit of peering through our windows at night to see who was there before determining if they wanted to come inside. We had run out of old materials to hang over the windows, so I developed a habit of covering my peripheral vision when I had to go into one of those rooms at night so that I didn't get shaken by looking out of the windows and seeing a pair of eyes staring back at me. I was especially trauma-tized one night during a thunderstorm when a bolt of lightning revealed the figure of a tall man staring into my brother's window. Mom seemed to know who it was and wasn't too alarmed, but to this day, I keep my shutters sealed and have night terrors during thunderstorms.

While we were still living with David in Independence, an old friend of my mother's was brutally murdered. Judy Spencer was only 21 years old when her body was found near an aban-doned schoolhouse in Salem, Missouri. It would take decades for the police to close her case. My mother had worked with Judy when we lived in Raymondville, and coming back to her old circle of friends and the small town rumors made my mother paranoid about what may have happened to her friend. It became a fixation in our home.

One thing about Dorothy - if she had an opinion, she made sure that you heard it. Mom was convinced that she had to speak up for Judy. She had wild theories about who would have done this and why. Soon, the speculation hit our circle in Mineral Point and names of people who I am not even certain had ever met Judy were being thrown into the accusation pool. Mom became certain that she would soon meet the same fate as her friend.

I vividly remember standing in our small yard and having a strange man call me over to speak to him. We had a fence between us, so I didn't feel afraid to walk over and answer his questions. I don't remember exactly what he was asking me, but I do know that some were questions about Roy. I was standing next to a soapweed plant and began nervously running my hands up and down the plant. Soon, I felt something wet dripping down my hand and realized that I had rubbed the edges of the plant so hard that I had sliced my fingers. This seemed to break my trance and I quickly ran inside the house.

"Were you playing with knives?" my mother asked in a horrified tone.

"No," I answered, "I cut it on the plant outside."

"Why were you cutting yourself with a plant?"

"The man made me nervous," I replied, "I didn't know that I was cutting myself."

My mom stopped and a horrified look came over her face. "What man?" she almost whispered.

"That man," I said, and pointed outside to the man still standing on the corner, now watching the kids exiting from the school bus. "He was asking questions about me and Roy."

Then, my mom did something that she had never done before. She walked me to a neighbor's house and called my father.

"Tell her!" she screamed into the phone. "Tell your daughter that she can't talk to strangers anymore!" And she handed me the phone.

"Debra Kay," my father said in his calming, flat tone. "Why were you outside without your mother?"

"I always play without Mom," I answered. This seemed to agitate him.

"How many times does your mom let you go outside alone?" he asked.

"Always."

"Put your mom back on the phone."

I could hear the yelling after I handed Mom the phone. Dad had come to see us in our trailer, and he knew that Mineral Point was not a safe place for anyone to be alone, especially not children. I had started a fight.

My mom would tell me years later that someone had "kidnapped" me from that yard and kept me for several days to scare her. When I ask my dad, he says it's unclear to him what all happened in Mineral Point, but he definitely didn't trust my mother or her boyfriend to keep their friends away. His theory is that they forgot me on the couch after a late-night party and someone let me stay until Mom came back to get me. His regret has always been that he spent so much of that time away from us, training with the Air Force, that he couldn't focus on getting more time with me.

ROCKY MOUNTAINS

And just like that, Allen was gone. The entire neighborhood was shaken up by his disappearance. My mother was a wreck. She was still making accusations against people for murdering Judy, and she didn't feel safe living alone. No one knew where Allen was.

After several days of anxious pacing, Allen's sister showed up at our door. "The police got him," she said between sobs. "They said he's going to prison for a long time."

My mother wailed.

Even though Allen did not officially live with us, my mother depended on him for so many of her basic needs - food, rent, transportation, and security. Mom still did not have her driver's license, and, as such, had no job. My father paid her $160 each month for child support, and she didn't have the money yet to file for divorce from David, so her only other supplemental income was from food stamps. While Allen's life of drug dealing and wild parties wasn't the safest option for us, she believed that it was the only option for her.

She also still believed that people were trying to kill us.

Shortly after Allen was arrested, my mother evacuated our small trailer and loaded us up in Aunt Louise's car to drive to take refuge with our family. There was not much room for us, as my grandmother and cousin, Keith, were still living at the house. We sprawled across the living room or on bedroom floors as we could fit.

Mom's fear of the world only briefly kept her isolated. My aunt soon found herself being the primary caregiver for me and Roy, and my grandmother's health was quickly deteriorating. For the first time in my life, I saw my Aunt Louise struggling with keeping everything in balance. To make matters worse, my Uncle Teet had severely hurt his back, leaving my aunt to be the only income provider for the entire family.

My brother still wasn't walking. I tried to help as much as I could, but I was soon to start kindergarten. Grandma Nervie's small stature and osteoporosis made it impossible for her to haul my fat baby brother around the house, and Uncle Teet's back limited how much he could lift Roy. My mom's presence was almost nonexistent. She would disappear for days or even weeks without leaving a clue about who she was with or where she was going.

"Something is wrong with his hips," my aunt informed my grandmother one day. "Look at how his legs bow out." To demonstrate, she tried to hoist my brother onto his feet to help him walk. He let out a loud cry. "And it seems to hurt him when he tries to straighten them."

"He needs a doctor," my grandmother suggested.

"Dorothy needs to take care of this baby," my aunt declared. "He needs a doctor and he needs his mother, and she needs to get this baby looked at now." Then, my aunt turned to me. "Sweetheart, how long have his legs done this?"

"They've always looked like that," I answered. "He never had straight legs."

"Dorothy needs to get this baby seen," Aunt Louise said again.

When my mother finally appeared some days later, Aunt Louise and Grandma Nervie relayed their concerns to her.

"It's because of the car accident I had," she said flatly. "The doctor said he may have some hip problems. He'll grow out of it." Mom didn't seem as concerned as everyone else in the room.

"Dorothy," my aunt began to lecture in a stern voice, "This baby is almost a year old and he still isn't trying to walk. Mama can't carry him and Teet isn't supposed to lift anything heavy. He needs a doctor and you need to keep your ass home long enough to take him."

Mom became defiant. "What am I supposed to do, Weezy? Give up my life? I'm 25 years old and I am stuck with two kids with no fathers. I deserve to get away sometimes!"

"They're YOUR kids, Dorothy!" Aunt Louise yelled back. "I love them, Dorothy, but unless you sign them over so that I can get them to a doctor and buy them food, I can't keep taking them for you."

"You are not taking my kids!" And with that, Mom rushed out of the house.

Almost immediately, Aunt Louise picked up the phone. "Dennis?" she said with a nervous tone. "Yeah, I need Debra Kay's military card...what? Well, um, no, I'm just helping Dorothy out...no, no, everything is fine. I just...no, you can't mail it to Dorothy. She's using our address..." And then she held the phone out while I heard my dad yell again from the other side of the phone. The conversation ended abruptly after that.

My aunt sat me down with tears in her eyes. "Debra Kay," she started, "You know how much I love you, right?"

"I do," I said.

"I want more than anything to have you here with me."

"I know."

"Your daddy is coming to pick you up."

I squealed with delight. "Is he getting Roy, too?"

Aunt Louise looked at my grandmother with concern. "No," she said, "I don't think he will want Roy, sweetie. Just you." And then, she asked me to leave the room so that she could talk to my grandmother.

Several days later, my Aunt Shirley showed up at Aunt Louise's house. She packed Roy's clothes and diaper bag and gave me a big hug.

"Are we going to stay with you?" I asked excitedly. Aunt Shirley had four children close to my age, and since they lived several hours from Aunt Louise, I hardly had the chance to see them.

"No, baby girl," Aunt Shirley said in her soft voice, "Just Roy."

I was horrified. "You're taking my brother?"

The aunts looked at each other. "Yes, baby," Aunt Shirley replied, "I'm going to take care of Roy for a while."

"But what about me?"

"Your daddy is coming to get you."

I became enraged. "You can't take my brother from me! Does Mommy know?"

"Yes, sweetie," Aunt Louise said, "Mommy knows."

"Then where *is* she?"

No one could answer me. I stood on the sidewalk, waiting for an answer. My brother started crying. I started crying. I watched Aunt Shirley load Roy into her car and wave goodbye.

"Wait!" I yelled as they began to drive away. "I want to give my brother a kiss!" I don't remember kissing Roy goodbye. I don't think they heard me. I can only remember standing on that sidewalk, screaming in rage and feeling betrayed by the people that I trusted the most. I felt enraged at my mother, who couldn't be bothered enough to stop this insanity. I was so mad that, when my father showed up that week, I couldn't be bothered to be excited to see him.

Life with Dad and Nora this time was tense. My dad's sister had moved in with the family to attend college, and Josh was nearing the infamous Terrible Twos. I was used to laughter and jokes at dinner, but now, our dinners were mostly silent. I wasn't enjoying my new school, and Nora wasn't enjoying my aunt's presence. Something was off with my dad, too. He would still soften when I climbed into his lap for my nightly kiss, but he seemed to easily become angry with Nora.

I spent most of my time playing in the Texas heat with the neighbor kids or listening to music with my Aunt Jackie in her bedroom. John Cougar's "American Fool" and Eddie Rabbit's "Horizon" are the two albums that bring me back to that era. I started using music to escape from things that made me anxious or nervous - my dad's blowups at Nora, my brother's toddler tantrums, and my growing anger against my mother. I didn't want to go back to my mom, but I didn't like the atmosphere in Texas.

I also didn't like living off base. My dad had decided to make the most of his housing allowance and rent a small home in San Angelo. Even though there were some military kids in my school and church, I didn't feel like I fit in. I didn't get the same sense of camaraderie that I had experienced in Delaware, and I missed it.

What I didn't realize was that my uneasiness was a direct reaction to my father's drinking. I didn't even know that he was drinking - I have no memories of seeing him drink at that age - but I have learned as an adult that children often feel the signs before they see them. I could feel Nora's animosity toward my father. I could feel my father's anger toward Nora. I had a sense that he was hiding from us on the nights when he came home late, and though I never heard them argue, I could feel the tension between them on the mornings after they did.

I was both sad and grateful on that day in December when my father told me that we'd be traveling back to my mother's immediately after Christmas. She was now in Colorado, living with my Uncle David and Aunt Linda. My dad's brother rode with us on the trip, presumably to share the driving responsibility.

"Why do I have to go back now, Daddy?" I asked sadly somewhere along a flat stretch of prairie.

"I have to go back to Greece," he said. "You can't come with me."

"Why not?"

"Because there are court rules," he explained. "You can't leave the country with me."

"But I did before."

"You did, but your mom and I were married," he said patiently. "When we divorced, a judge made rules about when I can see you and where you can go. And his rules say that you can't leave the country until you're an adult." My dad had a great way of explaining things to me in a manner that made sense - not like my mom's friends, who seemed to just skirt around answers.

I was amazed at the huge mountains we encountered when we entered Colorado. I remember that it was almost dark, but we arrived just in time for me to see the sunset over the Sangre de Cristo mountain range. To this day, the Sangre de Cristo is my favorite part of the Rocky Mountains, most likely because of my early memories there.

My aunt and uncle had moved to what seemed to me to be a giant house in Westcliffe. It sat on a hill that overlooked a ravine on one side and had a big mountain on the other. The house had certainly once been a majestic Victorian home, with french doors that opened to a wide patio and so many rooms on the second story. Even though there were so many rooms, my mother and I shared one room with my cousin, and my male cousins shared another. Two rooms remained locked at all times.

I celebrated my sixth birthday with my mother. I also celebrated the day by returning to school. I immediately liked this school - I was tested and put into a small reading group with kids who would really read. I started doing basic math instead of just identifying numbers. I didn't feel like a burden to the teachers when I wanted to opt for a reading magazine with words and not just pictures.

One day, I came home to find my mother sobbing at the top of the patio stairs.

"They took him away," my mother sobbed. "David has him and now I'm never getting him back!"

"Roy?" I asked while wrapping my arms around my mother.

"Yes!" she cried, "Shirley let that monster have him! He said I'm never seeing him again!"

Mom and David still had not filed for divorce. I heard the story from David himself some years later, and I tend to believe his side, given that I know how hard my aunt was trying to fight to get Roy into a pediatrician.

According to David, my aunt had been contacting the State of Missouri to get assistance for Roy. The state wanted to see guardianship papers and a custody agreement, neither of which existed. Roy was now a year old and still couldn't walk.

Crawling seemed to be agonizing for him, though he was quite cheerful doing all other things.

Finally, the state did a search for both of Roy's parents. When they couldn't locate my mother, they found David. David had been calling my mother regularly in Colorado, asking to speak to Roy, and I knew that I had to play the "Roy is sleeping" game when he did. I didn't feel right lying to David, but I remembered how I had seen him grab my mother's hair when she made him angry, and I did what she told me to do for fear that he would find her and grab her like that again.

When David learned Roy was with my aunt, he clocked out from work and made the 4-hour drive to her house. Aunt Shirley knew that she had no legal right to fight him, and she didn't try. Instead, she packed up Roy's things and started to see them out the door - but David wasn't going to leave that easily.

"Call Dorothy", he demanded. "I want to talk to her." Aunt Shirley was kind of relieved at the idea that she wouldn't have to break the news herself, and she dialed the number. David grabbed the phone before she could speak.

"Hey, Dorothy!" he said cheerily. "I'm just calling to see how the kids are."

"Oh, Debie is in school, and I just gave Roy his lunch."

"Oh yeah? Is he feeling OK?"

"Sure!" she replied cheerily. "He's just down on the floor right now playing, I'm just waiting for him to fall asleep."

"You're a lying bitch," David hissed. "I'm at your brother's house and I've got my son in my lap right now." And with that, he put the phone up to Roy so that Mom could hear his baby coo.

"PUT HIM DOWN NOW!" Mom shouted into the phone. "Don't you dare lay a hand on my son!"

"You're never seeing me nor your son again." And with that, David slammed down the phone and left to return to Independence with Roy.

My Uncle David had decided that the solution to my mother's broken heart was a new boyfriend. His friend, Bob, had just gone through a terrible divorce, so bad that Bob had tried to run his truck off a cliff to end the agony of the pain. By the grace of God or just by bad drunk driving, Bob's truck veered the other direction and hit a tree instead. Uncle David sent my mother to the hospital to cheer up his friend, and my mother enjoyed having someone to nurture back to health.

I wasn't very impressed with Bob. I didn't hide those feelings, either. Bob was exactly 15 years older than my mother (they had bonded over a shared birthday), with a long ponytail and full beard. He was tan from working in the sun each day, and even though he was shorter in height, his broad shoulders and large biceps were hard to hide under his flannel shirts and Carhart vests. He was a quiet man who wore thick transitional lensed glasses and was never seen without some sort of hat.

He didn't seem bothered by my disliking of him. He took it in as merely information, and never reacted to my folded arms or gritted teeth. He just continued visiting with whoever he wanted to visit with at the house, and though he didn't ignore me, he also didn't try to make friends with me. One day, I broached this topic with him.

"I don't like you," I said flatly.

"Well, I can't say if I like you, because I don't know you," he replied, reflecting the same flat tone. "I'm sure I would, though, if you wanted me to know you. I tend to like most children."

"I'm not like most children."

He laughed. "I have noticed that."

"Are you going to marry my mom?"

Bob choked. "Well, kiddo," he said with a laugh, "I've done that three times already, and I don't think it's a good idea to try it again. So probably not."

"OK." I had gotten the answer that I wanted, and I left him alone.

And they didn't get married. Instead, we moved into Bob's house in Florence.

I spent the first week or so throwing an absolute fit, giving my mother the silent treatment, and barely doing any chores that I was given. One day, to my horror, my mom left me at home with Bob while she went to work at her new job.

"Let's talk." Bob motioned me to sit down on the floor in the living room that he was taking a break from painting. "You see, kid," he started between bites of his ham sandwich, "I figure if we're going to live together, we'll need to figure out how to become friends. Got any ideas?"

I shrugged.

"Maybe we can find things that we both like. I notice that you like reading, am I right?"

I nodded.

"Me, too," he said cheerfully. "I read a lot before bed."

"You do?" I asked in amazement. I had become so used to my mother's friends being put out by my requests to have them read to me, and, still being in kindergarten, I was eager to learn how to do it better. "Would you want to read to me? Will you teach me how to do it better?"

"Sure!" he said with a smile. "I'll even help your mom pick out some new books. Do you like Dr. Suess?"

"I do!" I said. "I have some, but I've already read them."

"Fine, we'll start there. Would you be OK with me reading to you at night?"

"Sure!" I exclaimed. I had seen adults do this on TV, but I had never had one offer to read to me like that.

"So there it is," he said, "we've got our first shared project."

And so, Bob began reading to me at bedtime. He was always very careful to keep my bedroom door open and stay at the foot of my bed. I didn't understand his need to keep space, but I appreciated it. Some of my mother's former friends were always in my space, in a creepy and personal way, and I didn't like it. Bob seemed to understand boundaries that I didn't realize needed to be set.

I found myself wanting to do more projects with Bob. Soon, I was helping him paint the different rooms of the house, and installing new cabinets. When he wasn't working, he stayed busy with house projects. I liked being his sidekick in these projects. He didn't speak much when he worked, but when he did, it was to teach me something about angles or tools. I realized that I craved learning, and Bob understood this, too.

My first day of first grade came quickly. I loved it. I was put into a math group with two other girls, and we studied out of a book that was different from the one that the other kids had. We formed the same group again later in the day to read - and these two girls were just as quick at reading as I was. It was fun to be challenged right away, and I raced to our house behind the school as soon as the bell rang to tell Bob all about it.

"So you liked it?" he asked with a smile.

"I love it! I get to do real work, not just color and nap."

"Most people don't like school, but I did," he said. "I'm glad that you do, too."

"I don't want to stop going!" I exclaimed. "I saw some kids in third grade and fourth grade. Will I go that high?"

"Yes, each year, you'll go up one more grade."

"And how high do grades go before you stop?"

"Twelve grades," he answered.

"Is that it? Only 12 years?" I was disappointed. "Then do I get a job?"

"Well," he said with a chuckle, "If you still want to go to school more, there's always college."

I got excited. "How many years is college?"

"As long as it takes," he said. "Some go for two years, others four, and then you can also go for six or eight if you want to be something like a lawyer or a doctor."

I jumped up and down. "I want to go to college!" I declared.

Bob laughed again. "I want you to go to college, too. But first, let's do our first-grade homework."

Bob had helped me set my first goal.

When I told my cousins about college, they laughed at me. "We don't go to college," they said. "We're poor. We're lucky if we finish high school."

"Bob said I'm going to college," I replied obstinately. They laughed again.

"I think Bob is pulling your leg. Dad's already told us that college is for rich kids. Keep dreaming."

I told their dad what they had said.

"College?" he exclaimed. "Oh no, we don't go to college - we ain't rich!"

"Why do we need to be rich?" I asked.

My uncle laughed hard. "Honey, all that takes money. You'll be lucky if you marry a guy with a good job to pay your rent. Get them college ideas out of your head."

When I got home that night, I sadly reported to Bob how my family had dashed my college dreams. He put an arm around me and said softly, "You know, your Uncle David is my best friend, but I don't always agree with him. You're going to college."

"But how?" I asked in tears. "We ain't rich."

"We *aren't* rich," he corrected me. "The first place you're going to start is with proper English. And second, there are two ways to go to college - money and being smart. We don't have much money, but you are smart enough to go."

"How does being smart matter?" I was confused.

"If you're smart enough, businesses will pay for your college. They want smart people to go into business, so they set up scholarships. That's how I went."

I gasped. "You went to college? You aren't rich!"

"No," he said with a laugh, "But I am smart, and my parents are smart, and we worked it out. Just like you and I will work it out. But remember - no more hillbilly language. We start there."

I agreed. It would hurt to give up my family's slang, but it seemed like a fair price to pay to go to college.

Farm Life

When I tell people that I grew up on a small farm without electricity and that I walked three miles one way to catch the school bus, they immediately think that these were the most impoverished years of my life. Quite the opposite is true. Life on our Colorado farm was hard, and it required a lot of hard work from each of us, but it was idyllic in every way. From the smell of the fresh fir trees early in the morning to the clear view that we had of Pike's Peak, nothing was missing from our farm. Roy and I still smile when we let our minds go back to the time he spent with us in Colorado, and how free we felt as children exploring the southern Rocky Mountain foothills.

Years before meeting my mother, Bob had invested a small sum of money into a piece of land in north Fremont County, Colorado. Fremont County is most widely known as "Prison Valley", as the area is currently home to 15 prisons, including the federal prison known as "Supermax". This, in addition to the arid climate, may have been what attracted Bob to the area so long ago, as he had spent many years working in a maximum-security correctional facility before relocating to Colorado.

We started visiting the land on a regular basis, with Bob and Mom walking the area and discussing the ideal location for a house. Bob was heavily invested in real estate across southern Colorado, and it was known to us that the house we were currently living in was being rehabilitated to serve as a rental unit. While our life with Bob would be far more simple than any other life we had lived, it was also the only time in my childhood that we were not poor. Between Bob's full-time job, his real estate investments, and a small trust fund that his grandmother had created for him, Bob never struggled with money. He also never borrowed. The land was the only loan that he had taken out, and he made sure that it was completely paid for before we took the risk of building anything on it. Bob had plans to live without a telephone or electricity - he wanted absolutely no connection to any government entity outside of paying his required tax bill.

One afternoon, as we were preparing the Florence house for renters, Bob broached the topic of our newfound friendship.

"You know," he started, "without any electricity, you won't have TV or a radio."

"Yeah, I know," I answered with a slight pout.

"That means that you and I will be spending a lot more time together doing these projects."

"I'm OK with that," I said

Then, he turned to me with a serious disposition. "Listen," he started, "I have three sons. I've never had a daughter. I don't know how to raise a girl, but I want to be fair to you and teach you the things you need to know. I just..." he paused for a moment. "I just know how to raise boys, so I'm going to treat you like the boys. How do you feel about that?"

I already identified as a tomboy, so I wasn't sure what he meant would be changing. So I asked.

"Well, more than just building a house. You and your mama will have to help build the house because we need all the help to get it done. I mean like hunting, fishing, working on cars...I can't help you with your hair, but I can teach you how to build things. I can teach you how to strap on your boots and be the tough girl."

I shrugged nonchalantly. The truth was that I had more fun learning anything from Bob than I did playing with children my own age. I was losing ground on my determination to not get close to Bob - I would actually forget my vow to not like him until someone outside of our family pointed out how close we had become. Now, I was beginning to feel like our relationship was becoming a betrayal to my own father, who was still stationed overseas and had no date to confirm a return home.

"Do you want me to call you 'Daddy' then?" I bravely asked.

Bob stopped what he was doing and looked away at what seemed like nothing. "I have three boys of my own," he said while still staring away. "I would be heartbroken if they called another man 'Dad'." He hung his head down and I could see tears start to well up from behind his dark glasses.

"But I called David 'Daddy David'. Can you be 'Daddy Bob'?"

Bob shook his head. "If your daddy had just left you here, it would be a different story. But he didn't - he's doing an important job. But you," he now looked at me square in the eye, "you can be my daughter anyway. I have never met your daddy, but I'd be proud to tell him that I loved his daughter for him while he was gone."

With that, we shared a teary hug. But I still had no reference to call this man that I had come to adore.

"What's wrong with Bob?" he asked later that week.

"I don't know...I just feel like a first name isn't respectful. Can I give you a nickname?"

Bob chuckled. "How about Twerp?" That was his favorite term for me when we would pick on one another.

"But I'm Twerp!" I protested with a giggle.

"Fine. I'll be Big Twerp. You're Ornery Twerp."

"Why ornery?"

"Because you just are!" And he gave me a quick tickle to the side before we returned to our chores.

We moved a small, gutted trailer onto the land and set up a manual well system. The search for water on the land proved to be a dead-end, so we set up a tank on one of Bob's old Chevy trucks and hauled the water up the mountain weekly. Our heat source was an old cast iron wood stove, which I learned how to start and keep stoked nightly. Since we had no way to blow air through the rooms, we had no doors inside of the trailer. The project before us was to build a house around our trailer shell, then remove the walls of the trailer one by one.

A short time after moving onto the land, my mom saw a doctor for menorrhagia. She was often tired and in pain, and the doctor had no solution for her but to perform a hysterectomy. Now that I am old enough to read her medical charts, I recognize that my mother suffered from uterine fibroids - a condition that seems to be prevalent among the women in my family. Being that she was only 27 years old, she was terrified of what was happening to her body and the only medical option that was available to her.

I remember this surgery so well because I felt like my mom left for surgery and a stranger came home from the hospital. My mother's free spirit was gone. She began to get depressed, and with that depression came irritability. Bob chalked her behavior up to the early loss of her fertility combined with the pain of surgery and found more outdoor chores for me to do to keep me out from under her foot.

I was never much for hugs as a child, but I always loved the comfort of a nightly hug and kiss on the cheek from my mother. I was healing from the trauma of her leaving Roy and me with our aunts, and beginning to feel like we were a family again. One night, not long after her surgery, I came to my mother for my nightly hug and kiss.

"Not now, sissy," my mother responded with a shooing motion.

"But I'm going to bed. Can't I have a hug?"

"Stop it!" she snapped when I moved into her space. "Can't you just leave me alone and get out of my face?"

With tears in my eyes, I skulked off to bed. That was the last night that I asked for a hug from my mom, and I can't remember her offering one after that.

Mom had secured a job with Estes Rockets, and she had finally saved enough money to hire a lawyer to represent her in a divorce from David. Mom and Bob loaded up her car for the drive to Independence to attend her divorce and custody hearing, with my mother promising to return with my little brother. I stayed with my aunt and uncle until they returned.

But they came home without Roy, and with my mother in tears. I overheard her telling my aunt that the judge had called her a bad mother, that he would only let her see Roy in his chambers, in his presence. He had ostracized her for her bright makeup and high-heeled boots, for prioritizing her social life over the safety of her child. Roy was now 3 years old, and a medical examination showed that he suffered from displaced hips. The judge saw her abandonment of him at a time that he needed medical attention as child neglect, and had even told her that if he had jurisdiction over my custody case, he would take me away, too.

After much negotiations between lawyers, it was determined that Roy could visit us for a few months without supervision. The preliminary custody agreement would give my mother summers and two weeks at Christmas with Roy. That summer, Bob drove my mother to Kansas City, and she and Roy flew home together.

I was elated to have my brother with me again. He was a joyous young blonde-haired, blue-eyed healthy boy who could now walk and talk and even ride bicycles with me. Mom had planned an impromptu Christmas for us, giving Roy all of the gifts that she had been saving for him over the years. Best of all, Roy immediately fell in love with Bob. We became a trio on the farm, with Roy and I tending to chickens and cows while Bob worked on the house and rebuilt engines. I felt like our family was finally whole.

The joy seemed to run out soon for my mother. David had informed Mom that Roy had developed something called sleep-related rhythmic movement disorder - he banged his head against his headboard in his sleep. Roy's doctor had explained that this was not unusual for young children and that he would grow out of his head banging on his own. Mom just needed to practice patience and understanding with Roy, two things that I had not seen from her in quite some time.

At first, Mom insisted on waking Roy up during his nighttime fits. It proved fruitless, as he would simply return to hitting his head once he was asleep. She next decided that she would provide more pillows, hoping that it would reduce the noise. Unfortunately, Roy and I shared different levels of a very wobbly bunk bed, and any movement tended to become apparent when the bed frame hit the wall. Finally, Mom resorted to hitting Roy's head for him.

The first time that I witnessed her rage against my brother was horrifying. In just the way that I had seen David grab my mother's hair and hit her head against the bed frame, I woke up to see my brother's hair entangled in my mother's fingers, my mother with gritted teeth, and Roy's head being forcefully hit against the wall. I then saw Bob run into the bedroom and grab my mother's body to pull her off of my brother. Everyone but my mother was horrified at the incident.

From there, I tried to wake up before anyone else could when I would hear the familiar chanting of Roy's vocal cords and he began to rhythmically crank his head up and down. If I had time, I would jump from my bunk to his and hold his head still in an attempt to keep my mother from waking up. It didn't always work. Sometimes, I was beaten in the process of her trying to get to my brother. Other times, I fled before she could make it down the hallway.

Bob was not always home at night. His job was broken into three shifts, and the crews took turns taking one shift on several-week rotations. I feared the nights when he worked the overnight shift because I was too small to keep my mother off of my brother.

Mom's rage didn't stop there. Roy had proven to have a defiant personality, one that wasn't much different from hers. Her treatment of his RMD lessened his respect for her, and the two began having standoffs during the day. If Mom said "right", Roy turned left. When she would resort to beating him, he would grit his teeth and refuse to shed a tear. This seemed to enrage her even more.

I'm ashamed to say that I fell into my mother's trap several times. I was angry that she had become such a hardened woman, and I missed the mom who hugged me and reassured me when I had awful dreams. I began to treat my brother almost as cruel as my mother did. When we would fight, I would resort to slapping him. When he wouldn't do what I said, I would grab his arms and shake him until he agreed to obey me.

Fortunately, Bob interjected as often as he could and would take Roy and me out to fish at the local reservoir or hunt for coyotes. We loved guns, and we loved Bob's lessons in firearms safety. To this day, neither of us are fearful of a gun, nor have either of us mistreated one. These were normal tools that we had in our home, and we respected the first lesson that was taught to us: that these tools were designed to do permanent harm, and should only be pointed at something that we intended to kill.

After several months, Roy's visit came to an end. We were all sad to see him go home, and I had no idea that it would be the only time that Roy would see us at the farm. I don't know if he still had bruises from a battle with my mother when he returned to his father, or if he just outright said that he never wanted to come back, but the judge quickly learned of how Roy was treated at our home and denied any custodial rights to her. I would only share one more extended visit with my brother again, and it would be me at his family's home.

I loved life on our small farm. I fell in love with being outside, and I enjoyed tending to the animals. I learned how to build a barbed-wire fence, bottle feed calves, and saddle a horse. I became very engaged in Bob's seemingly constant project of tearing apart and rebuilding engines, and the science behind a Chevy small block V8 fascinated my young mind. Inside the house, I learned how to care for our kerosene lanterns and keep the smoke from the cast iron stoves to a minimum when building fires.

As much as I enjoyed getting dirty, Bob still enjoyed

spoiling me with the frills of being a little girl. It wasn't uncommon for him to bring home roses for me and my mother - a single red rose for her to symbolize his true love, and a pink or white rose for me to represent sweetness and youth. He was also very intentional about building my bedroom. He chose the north side of our home for me, and it was the only room that he splurged to invest in a set of small french windows. Once the room was complete, he showed me the joy of opening the windows to the fresh mountain air and the beautiful southern side of Pikes Peak. We spent many family nights in the living room, listening to country music on a small battery-operated radio, with Bob twirling my mother around to their favorite songs. When Mom would tire, he would grab me and teach me the basic two-step ("though they do it wrong in Texas", he warned me) and the 1-2-3 rhythm of a waltz.

My thirst for knowledge became insatiable. Much to my horror, my third-grade assignment was to the homeroom of Mrs. Ruch. She was known throughout the school for her strict disciplinarianism and high standards for her students. Even so, when my closest friends and I inquired about the older students in her class, they laughed and assured us that Mrs. Ruch was the most fun of all the teachers they had.

I had become easily agitated by the start of third grade. The excitement that I had for school had now become boredom, as I was able to quickly master the multiplication tables and grammar assignments that were meant to keep us busy for at least a full semester. I became restless. I began disrupting the class with my negative energy. To make matters worse, I was starting to develop in areas that none of the other girls had yet, and the boys took notice. I began to retaliate with physical violence.

Mrs. Ruch should have punished me in the same way that I had heard of her punishing disruptive boys, but she didn't.

Instead, she brought a small computer into our classroom and set it up next to my desk.

"You are the new computer tutor!" she told me one morning. "Your job is to learn these new math games for us, and then teach the other students how to play them. Can you do that?"

"Yes!" I exclaimed excitedly. And so, when I was done with my school assignments - often far ahead of my peers - I was to head to the computer and load one of the math games.

I learned long division and long multiplication. I began multiplying fractions using common denominators. At some point, the numbers started to be replaced with a small "x", and I figured out how to find out what "x" meant. I was having a blast - and best of all, I was no longer frustrated nor disruptive.

The time came for us to take our first standardized tests. Mrs. Ruch took the time to explain to us that these tests were just a task that we needed to accomplish and that we didn't need to study nor be anxious about what they meant. Our biggest struggle, she said, would be sitting still for the many hours needed to complete these tests. As such, she promised to spread the testing windows throughout the week in a way that allowed us to take a break from the mundane repetition of sitting in one place, filling in small circles.

The first part of the test was mind-numbing. I had regressed to kindergarten, where sentences were compiled partly of words, partly of small pictures. Other questions were formatted as patterns of shapes that I was to finish, without much other instruction. I took the advice of Mrs. Ruch and treated the test as one mundane task and did not get nervous about how I performed.

Several weeks later, I was introduced to a woman named Eileen. Eileen was not a teacher, she explained, but worked for the board of education and drove to our town from Colorado

Springs. She would be meeting with me weekly in a small janitor closet to work on more tests.

"What did you think about the standardized test?" she asked me.

I shrugged. "It wasn't so bad."

"Well," she said, "we're going to do another one, but this one has blocks and pictures. Are you OK with that?" I agreed, and we spent about an hour together with me finishing stories with pictures and recreating shapes with colored blocks while Eileen watched a timer. We finished, and I returned to the classroom while Eileen and Mrs. Ruch met at her desk.

Mrs. Ruch informed me that she was going to call my mother to the school to meet with her. Mom seemed put out by the idea that she had to take the time to come to school about me and made sure that I understood the inconvenience of this the morning of their meeting.

"Mrs. Wells!" Mrs. Ruch greeted my mother, "I'm excited to finally meet you!"

The presumption of her name only agitated my mother more. "Ms. Murdock," my mother corrected her, "And I prefer to be called Dottie."

Mrs. Ruch straightened her jacket and cleared her throat. "All right then, Dottie. It's great to finally meet Debra's mother."

"What did she do?" My mother had a way of cutting straight to the point.

"Debra?" Mrs. Ruch seemed aghast. "She's great! I just wanted to discuss what a remarkable student you have on your hands."

Mom seemed disinterested. "I didn't need to drive all the way here to talk about her good grades."

Mrs. Ruch got more serious. "Dottie, we have been

working with Debra on some things. Have you heard of the Stanford-Binet intelligence test?"

"Doesn't sound interesting to me," Mom said in a sharp tone. I was becoming embarrassed by her abrasiveness.

"Well, I called you here to discuss her results. Debra tested as highly advanced when she met with our test administrator."

"What does that mean?"

"Well," Mrs. Ruch became very serious, "her results are what some people refer to as a genius. Debra has a very special gift, and we'd like to work more with her to develop it."

Mom perked up. "My daughter is a genius?"

"Yes, you could say that," Mrs. Ruch smiled. "She's very special, even to me." She turned her smile toward me and winked.

"What do you need from me?" This time, my mother's question seemed genuine.

"We'd like your permission to let her continue to work with our specialist, Eileen. Our school doesn't yet have a gifted program, and I think the work that Eileen and Debra could do together would give us good information to pilot one."

"I like Eileen!" I interjected, somewhat to reassure my mother. "She comes all the way from Colorado Springs and she's very nice!"

"OK," my mom agreed. "What else?"

"Well, Debra tells me that you don't have electricity. Is that true?"

"Yes," Mom shifted as if she could feel judgment coming, "but my daughter is well fed, always has clean clothes, and stays warm." Her tone had become defensive.

"I understand that," Mrs. Ruch softened her voice, "but I worry about her eyes. And what about a refrigerator? Does she get fruit and milk?"

Mom stood up hastily and grabbed my arm. "I'm not

taking this shit," she announced.

"Ms. Murdock, wait!"

My mom turned on her heels. "If you're going to tell me that I'm a bad mother, you can go to hell. I'll take my daughter out of here so fast..."

"No," Mrs. Ruch assured her. "My husband Pete - he works for a computer company. I just think Debra would benefit so much from what he can do for her. Please, I have a full library at home and I was thinking if you don't mind, that I'd like to have her visit us." She softened again. "Please," she said in a low tone, "I didn't mean to sound harsh. I just...I see so much potential in Debra, and I love watching her mind be challenged in new ways. Will you consider letting her visit us?"

Mom pursed her lips. She loved having the upper hand like this. "I'll think about it." And we left.

I began spending time with Mrs. Ruch and her family at her house. Her entire basement was a library where I spent hours sorting through everything from classic English novels to biology textbooks. Upstairs, in the center of the living room, stood a grand piano, where I would teach myself to match the music notes on the paper to the ivory keys on the piano, testing with my ears if the pitches matched to make the correct note that I knew from music class. The best part, though, was the small IBM computer that sat on a desk in the guest room. Peter had loaded the same games that I played in class, plus a few extra ones that were even more complex.

Mrs. Ruch's mother lived in a small attached apartment next to the garage. She was a kind and lively woman, and I enjoyed visiting with her and laughing at her witty humor. Best of all was when she would get permission to bring my best friend to stay with me in the guest room. We had the most fun in that library, finding all of these books and bringing them upstairs to read on the floral blanket that covered the guest bed.

Mrs. Ruch took us with her one day to run errands at an organization where she volunteered. On the door was a big sign that read "United Way", and through the doors were at least a dozen people who seemed to gush over her presence. We were in awe. Everyone was so friendly, and they seemed like important people - some were even called "doctor"!

As we left, she explained to us, "The United Way is a large group that brings together people from all over the world to help other people. They have some people who build houses, and others who help to deliver food to certain countries. My work here is to help build hospitals in countries where people can't afford to have good medical care."

We were in awe. That day, in the back seat of Mrs. Ruch's car, my friend and I promised each other that we, too, would one day do something as amazing as what the United Way did.

That summer, a new family moved onto our road. The Eshelman's were a unique family - a hippie Christian family with conservative values and a modern approach to life. Bob became quick friends with the father, Bobby. The children were close to my age, and I was happy to have company at the bus stop. They quickly invited me to attend their new church, and I was excited to comply.

Kirkwood Presbyterian Church was a small country church with a playground and a vast array of Sunday school classes held in the basement. Our class was taught by one of the aids at our elementary school, Mrs. Mace. She enthusiastically taught us about the importance of Easter, the personalities of each of the original Apostles, and early bible stories of men like Noah and Abraham.

For me, the most important lesson was about how some Christians were forced to hide their faith. We were at the end of the Cold War (though we didn't know it yet), and the appalling stories of life behind the Iron Curtain were such a contrast to the life we were living in America. I learned about children who not only were forbidden to attend church but weren't even allowed to own a bible. I thought about what Mrs. Ruch had explained about the United Way and I made a decision - our church would buy bibles for families in these countries.

Someone found an old Cool Whip container, and before each Sunday service, I solicited innocent parishioners for loose change to buy bibles for children in Russia. I had no plan on how we would smuggle these bibles into the countries, much less where we would buy them, but I needed to do something and this was it. We kept the Cool Whip bowl in the freezer and brought it out each Sunday. Soon though, it was full, and I still had no plan.

"I think maybe it's time we find a way to use this," our pastor said to me one day with a grin.

"It needs to go to Russia," I declared firmly.

"Well," he said, scratching the bald spot on his head, "I do appreciate that effort, but do you know anyone in Russia?"

I didn't.

"And neither do I," he said. "So can we maybe buy a bible for a needy family instead? Maybe someone locally?"

"I don't think so," I said. "I told people that we were sending bibles to Russia, and that's what they are expecting."

He laughed lightly. "I think the good people of this parish will understand if we remind them that we may encounter some...exportation issues."

I realized that I was arguing with a man of God - a man who wore a starched, colorful stole and read the word of God every Sunday. I finally relented and agreed that he could use the donations as he saw fit, with the understanding that he explained to the parish why he was making that decision.

I wasn't allowed to create my own fundraising project again.

BACK TO CADET

Things were changing on the farm. It was a familiar shift, much like the one I experienced when I went to live with Dad and Nora in Texas. I couldn't hear the arguing, but I sensed the tension. It once was Bob trying to keep me outside and out from under my mother's feet; now, I felt like my mother was trying to get me out of the house more to be away from Bob.

Bob was drinking more than I had ever seen him drink before.

The cement plant where he worked had shut down. Even though he had a solid income with his rental properties and received a small trust check monthly, Bob felt defeated. He was obviously becoming more depressed, and his occasional indulgence in a few cheap beers became a daily routine of a case or more. He continued to work outside and on finishing the house, but he drank while doing it.

I didn't see what my mother saw. She seemed to be on edge when he opened the first beer of the day, and she tried to control how much he would drink. The more he drank, the more passive-aggressive she became. I was irritated at how much I observed her trying to control him. I couldn't understand why this was such a problem in her eyes.

The late 1980s saw the growth of the prisons in our area. When my parents learned of a large hiring event for correction officers, they began debating if Bob should apply. He spoke of his days as a correction officer with great pride, and he was highly trained to work in maximum security operations. The decision was obvious to me, but they each expressed trepidation about Bob applying for one of the open positions.

Their reasons were revealed to me one summer afternoon.

Mom was working, and Bob was more sullen than I had ever seen him be. I tried my normal antics to cheer him up - teasing him about his truck, asking philosophical life questions, but nothing was changing his demeanor. We began discussing his grandmother, and if he thought he would see her in heaven one day. His answer shocked me.

"Kid," he said, "people like me don't go to heaven."

"Why? Because you drink? Because I hope you know that's not true - God forgives everyone."

He shook his head. "I drink because of the reasons I won't go to heaven. Because of the things I've done."

I was confused. I'd never seen Bob do anything bad enough to make me not like him, much less for God to not forgive him.

Tears began to well in Bob's eyes. He looked down at his hands, which were clenched tightly.

"These hands...these are the hands of a monster." He began wringing his hands in a motion that was somewhere between washing them clean and tightening them. The tears in his eyes fell on his hands.

"When I brush your hair at night...when I hug you...I look at these hands and remember that I don't deserve to touch anything so sweet with hands that could murder a person."

I gasped. "You aren't a murderer!" I argued. "You'd never murder a man!"

"Maybe not, but I've killed one."

I thought back to his parents' many visits when they would pull out their slides and tell us stories in the pictures. I remembered seeing two photos of a man in a camouflage uniform - a man with reddish-brown hair with Bob's last name on the tag, who was too young in the colored photo to be his father.

"Was that you in Grandpa's picture? The Marine?" I thought that I was understanding more.

"It was," he said. "I was in Vietnam."

I breathed a sigh of relief. "Our pastor says that war isn't murder. You aren't a bad person, you're a Marine!"

Bob shook his head. "I'm not ashamed of what I did for my country," he said, "I just didn't like the way I was treated when I got home."

"Then what?" I asked, giving him a tight hug.

Bob began sobbing. "I didn't have a choice." He cried so hard that his large shoulders shook in my arms. I cried, too, even though I didn't know why.

Finally, Bob's tears began to dry. He sat me back on the truck bed and looked at me firmly.

"Kid," he said, "I never tell this story. I only told your mama because she wants me to go back to working in the prison, and she needed to know."

It was hard for young me to stay quiet, but I did it. I did it throughout the entire story. I listened to him tell me in broken pieces about how a group of prisoners overcame officers in different parts of the prison, how they held some hostage and beat others. He used words like "fires" and "bodies", and I don't remember if he wasn't able to tell the story clearly, or if I was unable to hear it. Then, he began wringing his hands again. "I saw a large man coming at me - I just knew he was going to kill me." He began sobbing. "I didn't know that I did it. I didn't know until I saw him fall, and my hands - they were full of blood and flesh." Then, he looked up at me. "I ripped his throat out. I took that man's life with nothing but my bare hands."

I worked hard not to gasp. "You had to," I said. "Remember how you told me that when you taught me how to use your gun? You told me that if a man might kill me or Mom, I had to kill him first. Remember?"

He nodded. "But I never intend for you to have to do it. That's why we have these pit bulls and German Shepherds - I never want you to know what it feels like to take a man's life. I'm a monster."

I felt defeated. I had no way to reassure this wonderful man that he had only done his job. I had no idea that I had just had my first encounter with post-traumatic stress disorder, nor how this one afternoon would forever change my life.

Bob had spent most - if not, all - of his career in the southwest. I have no information about where he lived and worked when this incident occurred, only the knowledge that he worked as a corrections officer in the 1970s and left sometime before 1982. My research of prison riots that fit these criteria has revealed to me some harrowing and ghastly accounts. It breaks my heart to imagine such a kind and compassionate person experiencing any of those events and living to remember them. I know that I only got part of the story, as I have learned that soldiers and first-responders never let us know the full details of what they experience. I remember sitting at that moment, wishing that I had a way to erase his guilt, and wondering if anyone else ever felt the way he was feeling then. I remember asking God to help me fix this.

Be careful when you ask God for gifts.

After a lengthy interview process and a difficult psychiatric evaluation, Bob was turned down for the position at the new prison. The hiring manager had told him that his skills were perfect for the job, but they felt that he needed more time before coming back into the field of corrections. He was informed that the area was being evaluated as a potential site for a federal administrative maximum prison, and encouraged to work with a special psychiatrist so that he could come back to apply for one of those positions. Bob declined.

Once again, I felt a familiar shift in my home life. This time, the battle felt more like it was more about with whom I spent my time than how my parents were spending their time together. Bob was continuing to find projects for us to do outside, keeping me from the angry wrath of my mother. When she was at work on Saturdays, he would take the morning off of his outside work to help me clean the house from top to bottom, meeting her seemingly impossible standards. Once there was not a spec of dust nor dirt left on any surface in the house, we would resume building whatever we were working on next. Mom would come home and carefully inspect everything on the list that she had left for me, almost in a way that she was looking for something to be wrong, but she hardly had the ammunition to direct her anger my way.

Bob, on the other hand, had started letting his drinking problems show more than he intended. He seemed embarrassed by the random stumbles and stutters that would happen after a day alone. Mom became keenly aware of this behavior, and began forbidding me to ride with him in the truck after a certain time of day, and kept me in the house after school. I was heartbroken because I wasn't bothered by his drinking, but Mom was furious that he was letting his depression get out of control.

One afternoon, she drove to school and met me in the

parking lot after the final bell rang. "Get in the car, we need to talk," she said sternly.

I was certain that I had left a toy in the yard, or forgot to dust something in the living room. Mom had a lot of stuff in the house, but she demanded that every inch of what she owned remained meticulously clean.

"When we get home, I want you to pack your things. Just enough to fit in the back seat. We're leaving."

I was confused. "It's not spring break yet, we can't go on vacation," I protested.

Mom sighed, a combination of irritation and sadness exhaling from her lips. "No, Sissy," she said. "We're going back to Missouri. I need you to tell your teachers tomorrow that we're moving home."

I panicked. "But, I'm having a slumber party this weekend, and I'm in the school musical!"

"No. We're going home. I've had enough."

"Enough of what?" I demanded. "What did I do?"

"Sissy, stop it!" She pulled the car over. "I can't do it anymore. I want to go home to my sisters. I'm tired of living like this." And she cried.

We had survived for years without electricity. Mom had a butane curling iron and enough light to put on her makeup each day. She had completed both beauty and barber school and was now working as a barber full time. She was so excited to pass her tests and to finally be out of the factories. And now, she was tired of it?

Bob wasn't around when I got home. I only had two backpacks that my mother would let me take, and there was not enough negotiating to get her to agree on letting my dog come with us. I cried with my dog. I cried in my favorite tree. I walked around to every cow, horse, chicken, and goat, crying to each one of them. I had never been more confused about what was happening, and haven't been since.

Two days later, we were on the road to Missouri - just me, my mother, and some useless things that she could pack into a 1982 Ford Escort. We were at the Colorado state line when she finally pulled into a payphone to call Aunt Louise, announcing our arrival. Unfortunately, my cousin, Keith, had just made the same phone call - he was coming from Colorado and bringing home a new girlfriend. The four of us, in two separate cars, were I-70 bound and destined to share the same small back room in my Aunt Louise's house. I can't imagine how distressing that week must have been for her.

It got worse. As soon as we pulled into Rolla, our car made a sputter, then a hiss. Mom pulled off into a service station, only to find fluid spewing from the bottom of the car.

"Yep, that's the transmission," the man who met us in the front announced. "We'll need to keep it here until we can get it fixed."

"How long will that take?" my mother asked in horror.

"Maybe a week, maybe two. Depends on how bad you broke it."

Mom was aghast. We were still hours from her final destination. "And how much will it cost?"

The guy looked again under the hood. "Maybe a hundred, maybe more. Won't know til I can get it up on the lift."

Mom shook her head. "I don't have time for that. Everything I own is in that car!"

He looked at our Colorado plates. "Can I give you a ride somewhere, ma'am? How far you goin'?"

"Not much farther," Mom said. "Look, I'll have my brother-in-law come tow it. I can't afford a few hundred dollars right now. I'm moving home and..."

"That's fine, but you'll need to get it out of here tonight," the man said sharply, realizing he wasn't going to get paid for this job. "I can't have stray cars sitting around out here."

It was almost dark when Uncle Teet showed up with his cousin, Joe, and tow straps. I was hungry, but Mom said I had to wait until we got to the house to eat. She burst into tears when their car pulled up. So did I, but not of joy - I wanted to go home.

Aunt Louise's house started as just a simple three-room home. Eventually, they added two small bedrooms for their children, and then a back living area and bedroom for my grandmother. One add-on bedroom became a porch, then a laundry room; Grandma's suite became a target for wayward family members. In less than one week, Grandma's old bedroom became a shared room for me, my mother, Keith, and his girlfriend, Dara. It was cold, cramped, and uncomfortable, and my aunt and uncle had hoped that this would be enough of an incentive for the adults in the room to make their way out - but Cadet is not the kind of town that allows for many opportunities to get out.

My mom found her own way to escape from the discomfort. Instead of a job, she found friends - her old party crowd. It was March, and my aunt was concerned about how much of my 5th grade year I was missing while my mom enjoyed her new freedom. Mom didn't seem to mind, telling her "Deb is pretty smart. She'll make it up later."

I was miserable. I missed the man that I knew as my stepdad. I missed my friends and my school. I had gone from learning Spanish and algebra to sleeping until noon because I had no reason to climb out of bed. The house was far from town, so I had no way of wandering into a library to satisfy my curious mind. My mom was now disappearing for days at a time. My cousin wasn't working, and I had become an albatross on his girlfriend. I sensed that no one had the heart to risk what would happen to me if they kicked my mother out of the house, and I had become keenly aware that she was using this as a manipulation tool.

Aunt Louise continued to push the school issue. Finally, my mom relented and drove to the school to enroll me.

"Nevermind, those people were no help," she announced when she returned.

"Why not?" My aunt was astounded.

"I need a bill in my name," she said with a tone of entitlement. "I need you to add me to something. They want an address, and my license is still Colorado."

"No." My aunt had been standing firm on her ground that my mother needed to get a job and move into her own home. She immediately saw through my mother's ploy.

"Weezy, I need your help!" Mom wasn't pleading as much as she was whining.

"Dorothy, you are more than capable of getting a job. The factory where you used to work is hiring and..."

Mom's entitlement cut her off. "I am not working in a factory after I worked my ass off to get my barber's license!"

"Well, your ass isn't cutting hair or paying the bills here, so it had better figure something out!" Aunt Louise's left hand slammed onto the table while the other pointed to the front door.

Mom turned to the door, then stopped and hissed at my aunt. "Fine. You don't want to help me? Fine! But that means that Deb can't enroll in school. Are you happy now?" And she stormed out the door for another multi-day excursion.

I knew that no one wanted me to witness these battles, but we were six people, crammed into a small house with thin walls. I also understood that no one wanted me to feel unwanted or unloved, but I did. I felt useless. I had spent so many years working on a farm when I wasn't at school or studying, and now, I was limited to just sleeping, sitting outside, and eating. I started feeling like my eleven short years had come to an abrupt end- I had nothing to look forward to each day, and I felt like my energy had been drained. My motivation to get out of bed was gone. Soon, I started wishing that I just wouldn't wake up. I wondered how to make that happen, and found myself praying for it each night.

I had no idea what depression was, but I was just starting my battle with it.

The solution that summer was to let me travel to Independence to stay with Roy and his family. David had since remarried, and they now had three children living in the house. David's wife, Debbie, was a large woman with a lot of sass and a big heart. I was excited to be with my brother for the summer.

Like my mother's family, Roy's parents were poor, but both David and Debbie worked long hours to make sure that everyone was fed, warm, and clothed. They had arranged their work schedules to be almost seamless so that an adult was always at home with us. The house was always full of games and laughter - not at all like what I remember leaving just six years earlier.

Once again, David had taken me in like I was his biological daughter. Debbie embraced this idea. The older children attended magnet schools - my brother was enrolled in a German immersion school, and Debbie's daughter attended a fine arts school. Debbie invited me to entertain the idea of staying here and finding my own school of interest. I was elated.

David and Debbie lived not far from a relative of my mother's, and the families remained very close. He and his wife lived in a big house in the country, with a pond and ATV for the kids to play. I was excited when we were invited to spend a weekend with them since he had been very close to my grandmother and I craved anything that could remind me of her.

On our first night at the house, we played games and puzzles and ate ice cream until we were sick. My brother was right at home, and he showed me all of the fun things that we could do over the next few days. This was exactly how I had always pictured my time with my brother should be. Soon, our uncle joined us on the porch.

"Well, Debie, do you like it?" he asked with pride.

"I do. Tomorrow will be fun!"

He laughed. "I hope so!" He put his arm on my shoulder. "I sure am glad that you're finally here with the family," he said.

And then, his hand slipped down. I froze. Just as quickly as the wave of horror blew through me, his hand was gone. I waited for an apology, but he said nothing.

"Well kids," he announced, "I'm off to bed. Sleep tight!"

I looked at my brother. He had been on the other side of the porch, and he clearly saw nothing. I looked into the house. Our uncle was kissing his wife goodnight. I breathed again.

Many years before, Bob and my mom had sat me down and had an uncomfortable conversation with me about good touches, bad touches, and not trusting anyone who made me feel bad. I didn't like the conversation when we had it, but Bob assured me that the day would come when I would need to know what to do. And what he had told me to do was to tell an adult. He explained to me that he would protect me from anyone who made me feel bad in any way.

But Bob wasn't here. My mom wasn't here. So I told his wife.

After telling her what had happened, she laughed. "Yeah,

he's a dirty old man, isn't he?" she said. "He's harmless. Get to bed."

I didn't feel better.

The next day, we did everything that we were promised we could do. We fished, rode ATVs, and played with golf clubs. At night, after a large dinner, we played games and laughed at each other's jokes. The kids in the room were having a blast. I started to feel bad about making a big deal the night before.

"Debie, Roy, come down here," the man's voice called from the basement. "I found something of your grandma's that you might like."

Roy and I raced downstairs to find our relative in a laundry room. "It's this box here," he said. "Roy, will you be a dear and bring that upstairs? I think there may be another one back here."

Roy grabbed the heavy box and started upstairs. I turned to follow him but felt a hand pull me back by the arm. "You stay here and help me," he said.

I felt my face flush. "I want to help my brother," I protested.

"He's fine." Suddenly, I felt my body get pushed up against the washing machine.

"But...the box?" I started crying. I felt those gross hands begin to cross my body, and then, I felt nothing. I still can't say where those hands went, because my mind went somewhere else. I felt rage and I felt numb at the same time. Not only did this man violate my body, but he did it in the name of my grandmother. I choked back my tears, determined that he wasn't going to get the satisfaction of seeing them.

My brother's voice lit up the room, and I was suddenly released.

"Yeah, we can't find it," the man yelled. "We're on our way."

I went to bed in tears. I wanted to call Bob, but he didn't still didn't have a telephone, still lived off the grid with no utilities. As soon as I had the thought, I feared what he would do. Bob was never unclear about how protective he was of his family. A surge of guilt came over me. Did I just wish this man dead at my stepdad's hands? Another wave overcame me. Why was I protecting him? I was confused, angry, and ashamed. As I struggled to fall asleep, I imagined Bob being taken away to prison for hurting - and possibly killing - our relative. I decided that telling him or my mom would be the worst outcome for all of us.

Early the next morning, I woke up to a heavy shadow standing over me. "Wake up, Debie," the familiar voice said.

I found Debbie's daughter asleep next to me and quickly rolled over to wake her up.

"No," he said, "let her sleep."

Nausea overcame me, and I started feeling dizzy. "But, you said it's time to wake up?"

"She'll wake up in a few minutes," he said, crawling next to me.

I felt my entire body crawling backward. "What are you doing?" I thought I had screamed it, but it came out in a tight whisper.

"I just want to cuddle for a minute." His hands grabbed my legs and pulled me closer. I felt something that I can only describe as myself being whipped out of my body as fast as I could go. I wasn't lying underneath him, but I felt him. I didn't experience what was happening, but I felt it happening as slowly as time had ever moved. His hands went under my clothes, his breath on my neck as his body weight held me down. I kicked, but it was useless.

The young body on the other side of the bed began to wrestle awake. The man quickly jumped to his feet, then left. At that moment, I wished that my out-of-body experience would last forever. I never wanted to be back in that body again.

I went through the next few days like a zombie. I began inspecting everything about my 11-year-old body that could have caused this. He seemed to like my legs, so I started covering them. I told Debbie that my shorts had gotten too small, and endured the summer heat in baggy sweatpants or too large hand-me-down jeans. My chest had begun developing early. I looked at my tank tops and realized how easy it had been for his hands to get into them. I asked for long sleeve shirts and baggy t-shirts.

Debbie realized that something was wrong, but when she asked me, I blamed it on the neighborhood boys. "They just look at me weird and I don't like it," I explained. It made sense to her. My curves were beginning to come in quickly, faster than the other girls my age. Debbie acquiesced to my desire to cover my skin.

Some days later, the man showed up at the house to pick us up for another weekend excursion. It was unexpected to me, and when I heard his voice in the other room, I felt myself fighting the urge to vomit. I ran into the bathroom and locked the door, sliding to the bottom of the door so that my entire body weight was holding it shut.

"Deb, are you ready?" Debbie's voice asked. "Everyone is waiting for you."

"I don't feel good," I replied back with tears. "I think I'm going to throw up."

She asked me if she could take my temperature, and I panicked. I wasn't lying, but I wasn't getting sick. I didn't want to be caught in my facade with no explanation as to why

I was curled up on the bathroom floor, shaking uncontrollably.

"I really just want to take a hot bath and go back to bed," I told her.

To my horror, the next voice was our uncle. "Debie," he said in a gentle tone, "Come on sweetie. Your auntie and I will get you some medicine on the way home."

This time, I actually vomited. I vomited so hard that my stomach heaved and my nose bled. David began banging on the door until he was able to break the lock open. When he saw what had happened, he grabbed me and washed my face.

"She's staying here," he said protectively. "Probably best anyway so the other kids don't catch it."

My mother decided that I wasn't going to stay with David and Debbie for the school year. She had finally been accepted into the local housing authority complex, so I could return to Cadet and finish school. The decision was made that we would make a family trip out of the drive back, bringing camper trailers and tents to stay at Lake of the Ozarks for the weekend before I had to return home.

The camper belonged to our uncle, so he and his wife decided that they would come along. My mom and aunt were looking forward to seeing them, so there was no way I was going to avoid being with them. I made a decision that I would stay with my brother at all times. I was certain that there was no way a repeat of the weekend at our uncle's house could happen with all of the other adults around.

We had camped a lot in Colorado, but this was my first experience in an RV. It was exciting to be able to make a tent outside and still have a hot meal for dinner. Even though I refused to wear my bathing suit, I loved the lake. Better yet, my plan was working - I was never within close proximity of our uncle, and no one noticed how much effort I was putting into keeping it that way.

The third morning came, and it was time to pack up our campsites. As I was walking toward the tents, familiar hands grabbed my shoulders. "Debie, I need help with dumping some of this water." I froze.

"I think Roy can help you," I said.

"No, he is busy with his tent. Just come with me."

I looked around. No one was paying attention to me, no one could see that the blood in my body had dropped to my feet. The hands pulled me, turned me around, and walked me to the woods.

Part of me wishes that I could give an accurate account of what happened next, but the rest of me is glad that I cannot. I remember standing in the middle of a group of trees, able to see the camper and hear my family, but no one saw me. I remember being turned around and seeing the zipper of my uncle's jeans come open. My next memory, though, is sitting in the back seat of David's car with kids on both sides of me, on the road back to my mother, wishing the car would run into the cliffs bordering the road so that I didn't have to open my eyes ever again.

The housing projects sat directly across the street from the local schools. Mom had nothing more than what we had brought in her Ford Escort, so we made pallets on the concrete floors with blankets given to us by various people. I had one pair of jeans, three shirts, and a shabby pair of canvas shoes with holes in the toes. I had never started a school year without a fresh, new wardrobe of well-fitting clothes. I had also never been bullied, but this was my year to start.

To make matters worse, Allen came back into our lives. He was fresh out of prison, and Mom was back in love. My tolerance for him, however, was only slightly less than none.

Allen's years in the prison system had jaded him against certain types of people - mostly cops and blacks. He made sure to reiterate this every time he contributed to a conversation. I wasn't allowed to make friends in the housing projects because the black boys would get me pregnant. He wouldn't allow my mom to give me stamps for my letters to Bob, because Bob had been a corrections officer, and everyone knew that corrections officers were just the cops of prison. I was disgusted at my mom's ability to ignore this, and I began to find myself enraged in their presence.

As soon as David was able to work, he moved us from the housing projects and into a shabby trailer in Mineral Point. He had strong opinions about how to control young girls as they hit puberty, and upon moving in, he turned the doorknob on my bedroom so that he could lock me in at night. On a rare phone call to Bob, I revealed David's bigotry and controlling behavior. I was grateful to hear Bob take me seriously.

"OK kid, do you have a gun that you can keep in your room?" he asked.

"I don't," I said.

"Is there a large knife in the kitchen?" Holding the phone, I opened drawers until I found a ten-inch butcher blade.

"I found one," I said.

"Listen to me - I want you to take the butcher knife and tuck it under your mattress. Keep the handle where you can get to it quickly if you need it. Don't tell anyone, not even your mom. You just keep it close by. Do you remember what I taught you, about where to aim if you ever find yourself in a situation where you have to shoot a man?"

I thought for a minute. "You mean his chest?"

"Yes," he said in a low voice. "Aim for the big part of his body first. Chest first, then head. Same with the knife. You got that?" I did.

We said goodbye. It would be the last time that I was allowed to call Bob, but it was the biggest comfort that I had since leaving him. I took my new comfort tool and put it exactly where my stepdad had told me. For the first time since we had moved into the trailer, I slept through the night.

My mother didn't seem to notice how Allen was beginning to isolate us from our family, but they did. Soon, he forbade me from visiting my Aunt Louise and pressured my mother to leave her job at the factory. I was becoming angrier at both of them. It wasn't unusual for him to yell at my mother to "get your bitch daughter under control." I tried to isolate myself in my room with my homework, but I was the only person outside of Allen that my mother saw each day, so she often coaxed me out to watch TV with her on the couch.

Allen's temper often flared. He would start fights with my mother that would follow her down the hallway to their bedroom, so loudly that I could hear the screaming in my room at the other end. One night, the screams became unbearable to me. I climbed into a recliner with our dog, Narek, turning the TV volume up as loud as I could. Over the noise of the television, I heard a loud explosion, and then, nothing.

I froze in my chair.

I listened for someone's voice. I waited to hear a sob, a curse word, or a door open. Nothing came. I turned the volume down to hear any sign of life.

After several minutes, I heard Allen call for me. His voice cracked, almost like he was crying. I didn't want to move. I waited to hear my mother call me, but nothing came.

"Debie, please, come here." Now I recognized the sobs.

Allen kept a shotgun on his side of the bed. My mind instantly went to the horrible realization that the explosion I heard could have been Allen using it on my mother. He called again, this time pleading.

I walked down the hallway as slowly as I could. Only a small part of me thought that I may have been walking to my death - his voice was so full of sorrow, though, that I doubted this was likely. I prepared myself for what I would see. Growing up on a farm had taught me what death looked like, but I had no idea what the impact of a shotgun shell would be on flesh. I paused when I got to their door.

I saw my mother's lower body laying across the bed, but her upper body was hidden on the other side away from me. I choked. Instinctually, I looked to the floor - I saw no blood. When cows are slaughtered, the blood rushes from their neck at such a pace that the entire ground floods quickly. If my mother's head had been blown off, I'd see the blood.

My trance was interrupted by Allen softly grabbing me from his kneeling position on the floor.

"I'm so sorry," he said.

I glared coldly at him. "What did you do?" My question was slow and calculated. It seemed to terrify him.

"I didn't mean to."

I looked at the corner on his side of the bed. The shotgun was still in its place.

"What did you do to her?" I asked again.

Just then, my mother's head rose from the edge of the bed. "Sissy, I'm OK." That's when I noticed that her neck and one side of her face were a deep blue color. It was then that I noticed the lamp shattered on the floor, with broken pieces of lightbulb in the center. Someone had either thrown or pulled it from the socket, which was the explosion I heard in the other room.

I turned my attention back to Allen. "What do you want from me?" I wasn't really concerned about what I could do for him but disgusted that he had the audacity to call this to my attention.

"I want us to be a family. I want to stop drinking, I want to stop hurting your mom. I was thinking that maybe tomorrow, you and me, we could go fishing or something. Something to try to be a family."

I looked at my mother.

"Sissy, please give him a chance," she said.

I had no choice. I had to spend a day at a river with this disgusting bigot, and, just like she did with her uncle, she was going to throw me into his lair.

The next morning, I devised a tactic. I tore a piece of paper from my notebook and wrote on it my name, my Aunt Louise's name and contact information, my date of birth, my social security number, and who I was fishing with. I folded the paper and tucked it into the front pocket of my jeans. If he was going to leave my body at some river, I was going to make sure that he went back to prison until his death.

The day was long, hot, and awkward. Allen tried to teach me how to bait a hook, but I already knew how. He tried to teach me how to cast, but I showed him a more efficient way. I was pissed that he chose fishing of all things for us to do since this was one way I spent weekends with Bob. To his credit, there aren't many other options when you are broke in southeast Missouri.

I tried to not intentionally push his buttons. He tried to control his temper. When one of us couldn't uphold our end of this unspoken bargain, I would shove my hand into my pocket and feel the paper safely tucked away. I quickly realized the irony of the day: as much as I was on my guard about him, he had equal trepidation of me. I realized that I was in control of the day, and, for the first time in over a year, I stopped feeling like a victim. I found empowerment in creating my boundaries and holding firmly to them. I was only 12 years old, and I had found the confidence I needed to pull out of the depression of my circumstances and develop resilience that would continue to drive me forward.

Allen was polite and calm that day, but he quickly claimed control once again. He found a farm job in Ironton that required us to live on site. We would be nearly one hour away from our nearest family member. Mom quit her job and packed our things, and we moved to a small one-bedroom home on the rural farm.

I was happy to help my mother unpack and make the house feel like a home. I had been given the bedroom, while Mom and Allen uncomfortably settled into an add-on room. I was happy to be in the country again, but I was uncertain about how I would fit into this new school. It was only early spring - just one year after I had been pulled from my studies in Colorado - and I was concerned about once again falling behind in my education. I pressed my mother to enroll me in the local middle school. She brought the topic up to Allen, who brushed it off with a casual "I need the car this week."

I continued to press the school issue. The district bus passed our house daily, and I was independent enough to get on it and enroll myself if that's what I needed to do. I said this one night at dinner.

"I've never met a kid who wants to go to school," Allen replied. "When I was your age, I would have been thrilled to be home all day."

"I like school," I answered. "I want to go to college, so I need to go to school."

He scoffed, "College? Seriously?" And then, he changed the subject.

I brought up school again later in the week.

"Kid," Allen answered, "we've got more important things to worry about than school. You could be out here helping me with cows so we can pay off the rent here."

I grew cold. "That's your job," I replied. "My job is to go to school."

"Do you see this shit, Dorothy?" Allen erupted. "Your kid thinks she's better than we are!"

I couldn't hold back any longer. "I am better than you are!" I screamed, standing up to make my point. "You never finished school, you dealt drugs, you went to prison, and now, you're stuck shoveling cow shit and can't even keep up with it. I'm better than that!"

Allen was now standing face to face with me, closing the gap in our heights with his head tilted down in my face. "You're going to sit down and shut up. I'm the man in this house."

"Bullshit!" I retorted. "Men don't hit women, and they don't treat their kids like trash!" And I ran into my bedroom and locked the door.

The next morning, Allen took my bedroom door from its hinges.

After Allen had left for work, I approached my mother with my new plan. "I'm calling Aunt Louise," I said, "And I'm going to live with her. You can stay here if you want, but it's been three weeks and I'm still not going to school. I'm not doing this anymore."

I expected my mother to argue with me, but instead, she quietly replied "I think that's a good idea."

Aunt Louise was there by the afternoon, and I was back to my old school. This time, I had enough confidence that I was no longer being bullied, but surprisingly found myself to be quite popular and making new friends. When the school year came to a close, I was in the social circle of regular phone calls and slumber parties.

One June afternoon, I saw Allen's car pulling into my aunt's driveway. "I think Mom is here?" I said out loud. We hadn't seen or heard from either of them in months.

We were surprised to find only Allen at the front door.

"Come in and sit down," my aunt said politely. "I have to admit, Allen, I'm surprised to see you here."

"I was wondering if you'd heard from Dorothy," he said. His face looked tired, almost defeated. "She left a few days ago and I haven't seen her. I'm worried."

I grew suspicious. "What did you do to her?" I asked harshly.

"Debie, I swear, I tried to make it work."

Aunt Louise composed herself in the polite way that she always did. "Well, Allen, I'm sorry to hear that," she said in a sympathetic tone, "but you know Dorothy - she can get headstrong. If she wants to disappear, she makes that happen. She doesn't check in with us until she needs something."

"Also," I added, "if my mother is running from someone, I'm not going to give her away." I glared at him from across the table.

Allen puffed his chest up at this. "Listen," he said, "I'm not going to cry over spilled milk. If she wants to leave me, fine. I'll find another. I just wanted to know that she's OK."

"I'm sure she's fine," Aunt Louise said calmly. "If she was in trouble, I'm sure the police would be here by now."

Allen stood up. "Well, since I don't have a reason to stick

around here, I'm going back to Joplin. You let her know that if she shows up." And with that, he left.

After a few moments, Aunt Louise turned to me. "Well baby girl," she said, "it looks like your mama will be back to get you soon."

I didn't want to go. I told her that I didn't want to go. She put her arm around me to comfort the fears that I know she shared with me.

"I'm not one to get involved in someone's parenting, but I feel like I need to give you some advice here," she said, softly kissing my hair. "Tell your mama what you want. It's time that she thinks about you. You are more than welcome to stay here with me, but I don't have the legal right to make her do that. So draw your boundaries and stick with them, ok?"

I hugged my aunt tightly. "I will, I promise," I said.

Several weeks later, my mother gave me the chance to keep my promise to my aunt. She arrived without a plan, just an order that I would come with her.

"Mom, I can't live your life anymore," I told her firmly. "If I go with you, you need to make some changes."

Mom became defiant. "Who are you to tell me how to live my life?"

I pulled my trump card on her. "I'm 12 now," I reminded her. "You and Dad have always told me that my custody agreement says that, when I turn 12, I have the right to tell a judge if I want to live with Dad."

Mom gasped. "You can't go to Greece!" she exclaimed.

"I can if I ask to," I reminded her. "I don't want to live in another country, but I also don't want to live with any more of your boyfriends, or keep moving around every time you mess up."

My mother slumped in defeat. "What do you want?" she asked.

"One school - until I graduate. No more men living with us. Whoever you date is your business, not mine."

"OK," she agreed, "but I don't want to live here anymore. This place is awful."

"Fine," I said.

"Would you be alright if we go back to Raymondville?" she asked cautiously. I found myself suddenly excited at this idea.

"And no boyfriends, right?"

"No boyfriends," she agreed. "I think it's time."

Houston - Not
that One

We made the move back to Texas County, Missouri with little more than our clothes and a run-down car. Mom chose the small town of Houston as our home base, and I started seventh grade with the confidence of a fresh start. I can honestly say that several of the close friends that I have today are some of the girls that I met that first week of school. I can't believe that this is a coincidence, but God's design.

Houston is a town that is very familiar with God. It is the kind of town with a church on every corner and down every back road. My friends in Cadet spent most of their weekends with their parents at parties or visiting family in prisons; my friends in Houston were busy with church camp and Sunday school. My life had definitely taken a turn for the better.

My mom stayed true to her word as well. She went to work at the same factory where she worked when I was a little girl and reunited with some of her old friends. She still remained her social self, with nights at the bar and dating men from town, but none of them came home and I didn't care about spending my evenings alone at home. In Houston, I finally felt safe again.

My father was in more frequent contact now, too. He had sent several cryptic notes over the preceding year to let us know that his job was keeping him busy on several missions, advising us to continue watching the news, but not revealing much detail. It became clear to us in late 1990 that my father was engaged in a military operation to protect Kuwait from Iraqi occupation.

It is easy to forget how the world gathered information in the days before social media and DVRs. In 1990, cable television was in real-time, and TV and radio were our sole means of instant information. Neither Mom nor I wanted to miss any information about my dad, so, my mother purchased a package of half a dozen blank VHS tapes that could each record up to 8 hours of television. We kept the TV on CNN, and before I left for school, I was to hit "record" on the VCR to begin taping whatever we missed. We spent our evenings flipping between live news and recorded news. It may sound silly or even neurotic, but watching the airstrikes eased our anxiety by reassuring us that our troops had the mission under control.

When my dad returned from the Middle East, he brought with him a new wife and two new daughters. My sisters became my favorite hobby. They were only 14 months apart, but they had such unique and vivacious personalities from the start. I discovered that sisters are very different from brothers. Even when they could barely walk, they were interested in watching me curl my hair and put on makeup. I had to learn early on that they were watching me at all times - every decision I made, every word I spoke. Even today, they are headstrong, successful, independent women, and they don't hesitate to seek me out when they need a solid perspective on their lives.

. . .

Mom found herself in a long-distance relationship that took her away on the weekends. My house became a weekend haven for my girlfriends, but with little risk, since we had moved next door to my mom's cousin, Janette. Jan was a surrogate mom to us girls, and her grown sons watched over us like bodyguards. Jan's youngest son lived with his father and attended high school at a rival school, but his unrequited crush on my best friend, Jill, brought him to my house on a regular basis. The absence of a regular male figure in my home allowed me to focus more on my feminine interests, and less on being a tomboy. Like most 15-year-old girls, I was starting to explore the world of boys.

Even though Mom wasn't around much, I still had strict house rules to follow. I was not allowed to have boys at the house without my male cousins present. I was not allowed to stay out past 10 PM, I was not allowed to date, and I always had to keep my grades high. My best friend, Jill, had begun staying at my house with me, and she followed these rules as well. Jill's parents lived on a farm far from town, and we both participated in debate and drama at our high school. It was easier for her to come home with me after practice and tournaments, and I enjoyed the companionship.

Every rule that my mother had set was broken with a fateful afternoon meeting.

Jan's son was old enough to drive, but he didn't have a car. A new kid showed up to his school and made fast friends with my cousin, and he owned a truck. It was the perfect ploy - the new kid wanted to meet girls, and my cousin wanted to see Jill. And so, unbeknownst to us, the boys were off for a Saturday adventure to my house.

I answered a knock at my door, expecting to meet a neighborhood kid.

"Hi," a deep voice said, "Is Debra here?" The voice was

coming from the lips of a dark-haired boy with the most mesmerizing brown eyes.

I froze. My cousin popped out from behind the dark young man. "This is Debra, that's Jill," he pointed. Except, he got us backward.

I extended my hand for a shake. "I'M Debra, THAT is Jill," I corrected my cousin.

The handsome boy shook my hand. "Nice to meet you."

As soon as our hands met, I flustered. I became embarrassed at my reaction, and, after inviting the boys in, excused myself from the room. I had been babysitting and used that as an excuse to take a shower.

When I returned, the boys were gone.

"Who was that guy?" I asked Jill.

She giggled. "His name is Myron Downey. He just moved here from Oklahoma. Isn't he cute?"

"I'm sure he's a jerk," I said in a disregarding manner.

Jill shrugged. "He seems nice. We'll find out soon enough - they'll be back after dinner."

I had never been a girl who was impressed with cute boys. I had discovered at an early age that the cute boys had egos, and the smart boys kept my attention. Frankly, I was disappointed in myself for feeling flushed by this one encounter. I decided to shake it off. I was the girl who usually let my friends date the boys, and I kept them as friends. I hadn't yet had a real boyfriend; I wasn't sure that I was the kind of girl who was even interested in dating. I wasn't going to fawn over this stranger.

The boys returned to find even more girls at my house, just as it normally was on a typical Saturday night. I observed Myron interacting with the crowd, wooing my friends with his charisma and stories of playing sports at his former school.

"Oh, so you're a football player?" I asked judgmentally. "Makes sense."

"I was, until the beginning of this year," he answered. "I broke my ankle in the first game and can't run anymore."

"I hate sports," I retorted.

Myron laughed off my cynicism and returned to his conversation. Jill was telling a story about a debate tournament that we had just had, and Myron's interest piqued. Jill was the cute and bubbly girl, with premature curves and a mischievous smile. She resembled a cheerleader more than a cerebral type.

"You debate?" Myron asked her.

I immediately became defensive. "We both do," I answered. "Is that a problem?"

Myron laughed again. He reached into his back pocket and pulled his debate club card from his wallet - the national card that we all earned after achieving many competition wins.

"Here," he said, handing it to me with a grin. My eyes grew large and I began to fumble with my words. "Not such a dumb jock now, am I?"

He probably should have hated me at this moment, but he didn't. On the contrary, he seems amused by my guarded nature.

I was now entranced by this enigma. He told me about his mother's death, the recent death of his best friend, and how he had spent the last several years living with his grandparents. He confessed to me that his dad was a truck driver and that they didn't get along, but he had to move here to be with his father after his grandmother started falling ill. I opened up to him about growing up without my father, how my mother was frequently absent, and that my dream was to find a way to go to college.

The night came to an end. After the boys left, my friends gathered around me with giggles. "But I don't even have a phone," I realized sadly. "What's the chances that I'll even see him again?"

On cue, my cousin popped back through the door. "Debra, Myron wants to talk to you. He's in the truck."

I nervously looked at my friends, who were nearly pushing me out of the front door.

I hopped into the truck to find the handsome boy wearing big glasses staring down at me. He nervously threw his glasses onto the dashboard. "So, I was just wondering, would you be willing to go out with me next weekend?"

My heart sank to my stomach. "I want to," I answered honestly, "but my mom doesn't let me date."

"Do you think she would if I asked her?"

I was shocked. Was he really now proposing to meet my mother?

He continued with "when does she come home?"

His persistence impressed me. "She should be home by tomorrow afternoon. But she's pretty strict so—"

Myron cut me off. "I've already talked to Jan," he said. "I know what she's like. I'll see you tomorrow."

In shock, I hopped out of the truck and went back into the house.

Myron arrived at my house promptly at noon the next day. My mother hadn't arrived home yet, so he waited at my cousin's house until she arrived. He was determined to make a positive first impression, and he felt strongly that being at my house with only us two girls would not bode in his favor.

I had just enough time with my mother to fill her in on what had happened the night before when Myron arrived to meet my mother. "I need you girls to leave us alone," he said in a very mature tone. Anxiously, I grabbed Jill and headed next door.

I returned about a half-hour later to find my mother in a surprisingly happy mood. "Sit down," she said. "I think we need to discuss boundaries."

She had agreed to let me go on a first date one year early, but only if it was a double date with my cousin. Jill groaned, knowing that she had just become bait. I was to be home at 10 PM sharp, and, even though Mom would be out of town, she would tell Jan to report if I met my curfew. Myron could stay a maximum of 15 minutes upon dropping me off, and only if my cousin was still with him. Mom would be home at noon the next day, and if the date went well and Myron wanted to see me again, he would wait until then to arrive.

Like a gentleman, Myron carefully followed all of my mother's instructions. Our small town offered little in entertainment, so our first date consisted of pizza and a movie. The only sign of his nervousness was when he commented that I had the cutest elbows; the small glimpse of vulnerability was adorable to me. We returned home several minutes early, and, after a polite hug, the boys left.

My first romance had taken off. It wasn't long before Myron was a permanent fixture at my house, winning over my entire family with his wit and charm. Though at different high schools, we were taking many of the same classes. He brought his homework to my house, after which my mother would feed us dinner and then let us take over the TV. We soon figured out that the food he ate at our house was often the only meal he would have. To remedy this, my mother purchased several boxes of Jiffy blueberry muffin mix and set me up each week to bake him a dozen muffins to take home.

If I were to outline the perfect first boyfriend for me, it would be Myron. He respected everything about me, including my stringent boundaries on personal space. Our relationship was based on hours-long discussions about our lives, our fears, and our dreams.

"What do you want to study in college?" he asked me one night.

I thought for a few moments. "I'm not really sure," I answered. "I just know that I don't want to live in a trailer park anymore, and I never want to be poor again."

He nodded. "I promise to do everything I can to make that happen."

"What about you?" I asked him, "You've never told me what you want to do after high school?"

Myron paused, then said, "I've never told anybody what I want to do."

"Why?"

"Because it's not possible," he said.

I scoffed. Everything about that statement was contrary to what I was raised to believe. I told him so.

"Well," he replied with a sigh, "do you promise to not tell anyone?"

I was surprised by his question, but answered "of course."

"I want to be a cop," he said quickly. "I've always wanted to be a cop. I want to work on drug and child abuse crimes."

"Why is that a secret?" I asked naively. "I think that's a cool job!"

He hung his head. "Because kids like me don't put people in jail. We're the ones who go to jail."

I grabbed his hand, and repeated back to him "I promise to do everything I can to make that happen."

Myron and I had no concept of what we were doing or how we were doing it, which was probably best because we had no fear of what was before us. His dad had left town and Myron made the decision to stay with us. My mom was beginning to fall back into her partying ways, and, after a frightful encounter with one of her drunk friends in my bedroom, Myron decided that we would move into a studio apartment on our own. He was worried for my safety and his future, and this was the only option that he could see to keep us on the right track.

Surprisingly, we had the support of our friends, teachers, and most of the adults in the community. His father's abusive behavior had become known to those in our circle, and my mother's negligence had reached new heights. Some members of my family gave Myron a night job at their turkey call factory, and, since his dad had taken the truck back to Oklahoma, my friend's dad cosigned for Myron's first car. We had defaulted to a survival mode, but it was the only way we knew to operate. Myron would tell me later that our years in that apartment were the happiest of his life.

Even though he had little money to save, Myron managed to buy me a small promise ring. It was a 14 karat gold band with two small diamonds, but I wore it like it was worth a million dollars. Myron made his intentions with me very clear: I was going to be his wife one day. He had no timeline, no hurry to make this come true, but he was fixated on the idea. Quite frankly, the idea frightened me. I had come to understand the great mistake that my parents had made by becoming young parents, and I didn't want to repeat that pattern in my life. Myron promised that he would never let that happen, that he would always make sure that I went to college and got out of poverty, out of Texas County, and became my own person.

Working full-time and going to high school was not easy on this young man, and late in his senior year, our guidance counselor advised him that he was a half-credit short of graduating, per our school's standards. The blow hit him hard. We had come too far to give up, and now, he felt defeated.

I decided to take on his fight.

I was a teacher's aid for the school's athletic director, which meant that I spent an hour each day in the office next door to our guidance counselor. The day after Myron received the letter denying his graduation, I went to the counselor's office and closed the door.

"You're making a mistake," I said, sitting down across from the counselor. He looked up at me with a puzzled look on his face.

"Debra? Is everything OK?"

"No," I answered, pushing the letter across his desk. "This is wrong."

He sat back in his chair. "Debra," he started, "Myron missed an entire semester of school and never made up his work. He's one-half credit shy of meeting this school's criteria for graduation. I'm sorry, but the rules are the rules."

"Did you tell him before now?" I asked.

"Well, no. We trust that the students and their families are keeping track of their own progress."

"I am Myron's family, and let me tell you what life in our house is like," I started. "We wake up at 6 AM and are at school by 7, where we go immediately to debate team practice. Then, we go to class until 3, after which Myron and I spend a half-hour doing as much homework as we can until he has to leave for his 4 PM shift at the factory. Myron works 10 hour days, 4 days each week. If we haven't finished our homework, he does it for an hour after he gets home. On Fridays, we board a bus to compete on our debate team, and we're home after midnight on Sunday. Since he's gotten no more than 4 hours of sleep each night, he spends most of Sunday sleeping and catching up on whatever schoolwork he couldn't finish during the week.

That's how dedicated he is to completing his education, but surviving is his priority."

The counselor let out a sigh. "I had no idea," he said. "I knew that Myron was emancipated from his family, but I had no idea that he's struggling that hard."

I leaned in to make my next point. "College is about ambition and determination, is it not?"

He nodded his head. "You could say that."

"Myron has big ambitions. He can't do it without his education."

"There is always the GED..."

I stood up with a huff. "A GED implies that he couldn't do the work. He IS doing the work. He has a 3.0 and his ACT is above average. He's worth more than an equivalency test." And then, I smartly scoffed at him, "Isn't the state's graduation requirements only 22 high school credits?"

"Yes."

"And Myron has 23.5 credits?"

"Yes."

"So if a GED is supposedly good enough for those who can't meet basic state standards, how is coming above state standards a bad enough outcome to require a GED in absence of graduation?"

"Debra," he sighed, "We have rules in this district. The rules state that Myron needs 24 credit hours to graduate, and I can't make exceptions to that rule. It's just basic math."

"No," I retorted. "Basic math tells me that if I round up, 23.5 becomes 24. And my transcript doesn't have a space for a decimal. If you really want to show this community that this school is about success stories, you'll apply the same rule." And I left.

That afternoon, Myron was called into the guidance counselor's office, where he was informed that he would be graduating that spring.

Colleges came calling quickly enough. We had continued to compete in debate, and I was a successful contender. Additionally, my grades and ACT scores were among the highest in my school, and I had experienced great success on the academic team and in music competitions. It soon became apparent that my concern wouldn't be if I went to college, but where.

Myron had his sights set on the criminal justice program at Southwest Missouri State University. He was one year ahead of me in school, but, since he didn't have the scholarship opportunities that I did, he chose to take a gap year to save money and wait for me to graduate from high school. I chose Southwest Baptist University, a private university close to SMSU that was home to one of the leading debate teams in the country. After many starts and stops, we headed off to our next chapters.

My expectations of college fell flat within a week of living on campus. I had lived in my own apartment for years, only seeing my mother when she could sneak over to do our laundry (she snuck it back into our living room when we weren't home). Now, I had to sign in and out of a front office each time I wanted to do anything short of going to class. To make matters worse, Myron could only visit me in our commons area with at least a dozen other girls around us. We were discouraged from going on dates alone. We had spent the last four years living alone, and now, we were being supervised at every angle.

I did find myself flourishing on the college debate team. At my first collegiate tournament, my partner and I took first place in duo improvisational acting. I had a natural talent for acting, but it wasn't my favorite pastime. I was actually quite disappointed that I wasn't keeping up with the rest of the team in forensics, and the stress of the pressure that I felt began to wear on my body. To make matters worse, Myron and I were drifting apart. He had found new freedom at college - freedom that he was never allowed to have as a teenager. He was smart, handsome, and witty, and being relieved of the obligations of rent payments and a full-time job left him with a lot of energy to finally be a young kid. While I was under the strict guardianship of a Southern Baptist administration, Myron was experiencing the nightlife of college. After nearly five years of being the centers of one another's worlds, we broke up.

The devastation of my first heartbreak coupled with the pressures of academic perfection led me to my first anxiety attack. I had no idea what was happening and felt embarrassed when the campus nurse diagnosed it.

"It's fine," she reassured me. "It's common with freshmen. You're away from home, life is changing, and it can be a lot to overcome."

But I wasn't fine. As a matter of fact, I barely wanted to get out of bed. To make matters worse, the factory where my mother had worked for so many years had just closed its doors. My mother was living on a small unemployment check and food from the local St. Vincent de Paul pantry. I decided to hang up my college dreams and move back to my mother's run-down trailer in Texas County.

I took two jobs to help my mother, but, to her credit, she never asked for money from me. I would race to the landlord's house on the first of the month to pay rent and beat my mother to the electric company to pay the utility bill. As often as I had seen my mother rely on our family when she could have done things herself, I was not expecting that she would be too proud to accept help from her daughter when she actually needed it.

Things were changing with my father, too. He had left the Air Force and was living with his family in Texas. We were in touch regularly, but the conversations were unsettling to me. My father seemed distant and sometimes irrational. I was surprised one night by a late call from him.

"I just needed to hear a kind voice," he said. But I could barely make out what he was saying through a loud blaring of music in the microphone.

"Daddy? Where are you?"

"Just out with some friends," he said. "It's been a hard day."

"Are you OK?"

"I am sweetie," he slurred. "I just wanted to say I love you."

"I love you too, Dad." And then, he hung up.

The next day, I confronted my mother.

"Mom," I said, "I think Dad has a drinking problem."

My mother looked at me with a wave of compassion and sadness. "Yes, baby," she said softly. "He always has."

I was shocked. "How long has he been drinking?" I demanded.

"It's been since he and I were married," she said. "So at least 20 years."

"Why didn't you tell me?"

"Because baby, you shouldn't ever think badly of your dad. I knew you'd find out soon enough, but I didn't need you to know too soon. He's still your dad."

My dad's late-night calls continued, and I soon learned that he had moved out of his house and was living with a recently divorced coworker. With his marriage on the rocks, his drinking escalated to a daily event. I, too, was struggling in Texas County. I was unhappy with my mundane job, and, quite frankly, felt lost without Myron. He called regularly to check on me, and we even met on occasion for breakfast, but the boundaries had been made clear to me. We were merely friends.

I made one final attempt to salvage my first relationship. I drafted a heartfelt letter and mailed it to him. One week later, I received a reply.

I couldn't read the letter. I wanted it to say "let's make this work", but I worried that he would tell me that we were better off as friends. Instead, I gave the letter to Jill and made her read it.

She folded the letter and let out a sigh. "It's not good news," she said.

"What? What isn't good news?" I demanded.

"Well," she said, "he did get into the highway patrol academy. He starts this spring."

"That's great news!" I squealed.

"Debra, he's also getting married."

I felt the blood drain out of my body. "He's what?"

She sat down next to me and put her arm around me. "He says he met the woman that he wants to spend the rest of his life with. They're getting married in August."

I tore the letter from her hands and raced outside. I had to read these words for myself. And then, I threw up.

I can't remember how long my emotional meltdown lasted. I remember trying to cry and being out of tears, and dry heaving once all of the liquid left my stomach. And then, in a moment of lucidity, I went to the phone to call my father. "Daddy," I said, "I want to come to Texas."

HOUSTON - THE OTHER ONE

I am self-aware enough to realize that the impulsive decisions that I make in reaction to my emotions tend to be the worst decisions of my life. Texas is the exception. Today, when people ask me where "home" is, I answer with "it's complicated, but I consider myself a displaced Texan."

I drove from Houston, Missouri to Houston, Texas on a hot day in May. I chose the route through Oklahoma since my car was notoriously unreliable and I wanted to always be near a payphone. As soon as I hit the Oklahoma border, the skies turned dark and the wind began to howl. I turned on the radio to learn that the entire state was under a tornado warning.

"Just drive," my dad instructed me when I stopped to call. "The storms are behind you, just get in the car and keep going. Don't stop until you get to Dallas."

And that was how my move to Texas went - I was literally chased out of Missouri and Oklahoma by dark, deadly clouds. I couldn't have created a better literary picture of the start of my new life than this.

Dad was now living with a work colleague who had just

been through his own divorce and was starting over as a middle-aged single man. I found myself in a "My Two Dads" situation, with both men scrutinizing every element of my clothing choices, social life, and every other decision a 21-year-old girl may try to make. Even so, their newfound bachelorhood left some element of fun. My dad introduced me to the nightlife of town; his roommate introduced me to Red Dirt music.

I discovered myself in Houston. Like Myron's college experience, I was finally free to be a fun-loving young woman. I could stop being guarded and uber-responsible and could start having fun with life. Also, I discovered the power that an attractive and intelligent woman can yield in the world. I took a small job as a hostess at a nightclub and spent whatever spare time I had singing with local bands.

The stage became my comfort zone. I had inherited enough curves from both Dorothy and Sandy to make me self-conscious, and it didn't help that they were planted on a short body with an inherently small stature. I hated the attention that my voluptuous body got me in life; I even blamed it for why my uncle had violated me at such a young age. On a stage, though, those curves got the attention of the crowd just long enough for my voice to mesmerize them. The first taste of my power on stage was intoxicating. Even though I was grossly uncomfortable talking to people one-on-one, I loved dressing up in red lipstick and leather pants, and, as soon as the women became angry to see the room's attention turn to me as I climbed on stage, winning them over with the first notes of a Patsy Cline song. My focus was on my business mind and natural talent, but I understood that I had to turn heads if I wanted to get through a booking agent's door.

I didn't have to struggle to find the party scene. My dad was spending each night at the club where I worked, which was convenient to him because it guaranteed that he would have a sober ride home at the end of the night. On my nights off, he taught me how to shoot tequila ("no chaser, you're a Wells") and swindle money from the men off the pool table. He wasn't happy about my growing fan base, and the attention I was getting only made him more determined to keep our social circles closely entangled.

It was somewhere around this time that I had my first severe health scare. I had started experiencing severe stomach pain regularly. I had always had bad menstrual cramps, but this pain came on quickly and would knock me to my knees. One day, the pain was so severe that I couldn't walk at all. I crawled into the bathroom to find untimely blood in my pants. I called my dad, and we raced to the hospital, where I was told that I had a torsioned ovarian cyst that needed to be removed immediately. I was prepped for surgery, and, on my way to the operating room, I saw my doctor grab my father's hand while he said "It's ok, Dad. I'll do everything that I can to make sure she can still have grandbabies for you." As the panic struck me, the anesthesia took over and I was out.

It didn't take my father long to fall in love again. This time, his sights were set on a beautiful, younger Hawaiian divorcee with two children who were close to the same ages as my sisters. We all liked her, and her children immediately took to me as an older sister. The romance would have been perfect, but for Dad's drinking.

Sadly, my sisters were not sheltered from Dad's alcoholism the way that I had been. My infrequent visits allowed him to hide his issues from me; my sisters had grown up in a house with his erratic behavior and violent outbursts. As such, it was not as shocking to them when my father hit his rock bottom.

We had taken my sisters to a local boardwalk restaurant to celebrate a birthday. My father had been agitated all day. Normally, being with his daughters was enough to break his foul moods, but that day was different. He was snappy all through dinner, even picking at the birthday celebrant and making snide comments to the rest of us.

I don't remember what finally set him off. I don't even think I saw the initial outburst that occurred as we walked to the car. What I did see when I turned around was a group of men wrestling my father to the ground, and I heard him yelling threats at us and calling us names. We jumped into the car and raced home crying.

When I arrived at the house with my sisters, the phone was already ringing.

"Get your ass back in the car and come pick me up," my father's voice growled. I hung up the phone.

It rang again.

"You bitch! Don't you ever hang up on me–" Click.

I called my sisters' mother and told her that she needed to pick up the girls. She was frantic, even after I reassured her that they were safe and my father was still at least 20 miles away.

Knowing that their mother was on her way to us, I took the phone off the hook. I went into the living room to find my young sisters huddled together in tears.

"I hate him!" one of them screamed. "I hate everything about him!"

"No!" I protested, "You don't hate Daddy! You hate what he does, but you don't hate him!"

My other sister sobbed. "Deb, there's nothing that we can do. I don't know what to do!"

I remembered that my sisters had just begun attending church. I thought back to my days at Kirkwood Presbyterian and asked myself, what would my church family tell me to do?

I shared an idea with my sisters. "We should pray," I said. They looked shocked. We didn't pray as a family, we didn't even talk about God. But, like me, they felt helpless and didn't know what else to do.

"What should we say?" one asked.

"Whatever comes out," I said. And so, the three of us kneeled at the couch, me between each of them, holding their shaking little hands. And each of us let the tears and the words and the hurt come out until we each couldn't sob anymore.

Afterward, one looked at me and asked, "Do you think it will work? Do you think Daddy will quit drinking?"

The other one answered her, "I feel like he already has."

The next morning, my father announced that he was going to the bar. My heart sank. He must have heard it hit the floor, because he said, "I just have to say goodbye to it." And that Sunday was the last day that my father had a drop of alcohol. He took two weeks of sick leave and detoxed at home, and then focused on repairing his new relationship. My sisters had witnessed their first miracle.

Watching my father work on sobriety for the first time in over two decades inspired me to return to church. I joined First Presbyterian Church, and my family joined me on the warm November day that I was baptized. I started counseling with the pastor and joined the church choir. I was still playing gigs in the bars and attending live music concerts, but I always made a point to roll my sleepy self out of bed on Sunday morning and join my new church family.

I also left my job at the bar for my first real office job. My dad had a friend that owned a CPA firm, and I became a receptionist. I was quite an addition to this crew - nearly all of my clothes showed my belly or my cleavage, and I don't think I owned a pair of flats that weren't cowboy boots. The office manager informally adopted me and helped me design a more office-appropriate wardrobe for the 45 hours that I would spend being the face of the firm.

My pastor happened to be a client of the CPA firm. He was surprised to see me at the reception station when he came in for his year-end tax planning. Two short days later, he returned with an envelope.

"Debra," he said, "the women's group has a small fund that they are required to spend before the end of the year. This year, they prayed, and your name came to them. Here." He handed me the envelope, which contained a check for $250.

I gasped. "This is enough to put down on tuition next semester!" I exclaimed.

"Oh, are you going back to college?" he asked.

"Yes, I need $750 for tuition and another $200 for books. This is going to help me get on a payment plan. Thank you!"

As I hugged him, he pulled me back and chuckled. "Don't spend that on tuition," he told me. "We have a scholarship fund that pays $1,000 each semester to a member of the church. But, we don't have any college students left in our membership. Apply for the scholarship. Use this money for something special for you!"

I nearly fainted. He had no idea that I had been praying for a way to get back to college. We hadn't talked about that in our spiritual sessions. I had never told anyone that I was worried about how I was going to do this and that I had planned to literally take one class at a time at the local community college until I could prove my academic worth again.

And so, thanks to the prayers answered by the First Presbyterian Church, I was a college student again.

. . .

The accounting firm where I worked was alive with women at all points of their careers. We were led by a vivacious young entrepreneur who was living out her dream of creating a work environment that provided a balance for young mothers and non-traditional college students. Not that we didn't have men in the firm - we actually had two very smart male CPAs who also specialized in trust management. They spent a lot of time laughing and shaking their heads at the random lunchroom topics that their dozen or so female colleagues entertained.

It was common fun for the married women of the office to identify single bachelors in the community and target them as love interests for us younger ladies. It also helped that they had some financial history on many of the local young men. When an up-and-coming entrepreneur would show up at the office for a meeting, these women would prod one of us to bring him coffee or water, and put a bug in our ear such as "his mother tells me he's not seeing anyone". It was entertaining, but none of us took them seriously. Besides, my interest was bad boys. I was attracted to the type that could keep up with my busy nightlife and sleep all day while I worked and caught up on my studies. After enduring my first heartbreak, I had no interest in a real romance.

"Girls!" our boss sang one day as she floated through the office door, "I just saw on my calendar that Michael Knight is coming in to set up a bookkeeping engagement. You're going to love him!"

One girl's head popped up. "You mean the lawyer's son?"

"Yes, that's the one!"

Another girl twisted her hair. "I saw him just the other day. I thought he was going into the Army?"

"Nope," the firm partner replied, "His mom told me that he decided not to sign his ROTC contract and finished his business degree instead. He's starting a landscape business."

I felt lost.

"Who?" I asked.

"His dad is the attorney in the office next door," Twisted Hair replied, "You've met him."

I shrugged. "Good luck!" I said to the girls. They giggled. It was going to be a big day.

That afternoon, a big personality with bigger dimples and glistening blue-green eyes waltzed into our lobby. "Mine!" Twisted Hair growled at me in a harsh whisper. "I get this one!"

I decided to focus on filing while she made her move.

After he left, his new bookkeeper rushed into the front office. "He's coming back tomorrow!" she said to Twisted Hair. "He signed the engagement letter! And girl, he's already making money hand over fist!"

I was the only person in the front office when Michael arrived the next day. I was surprised by his easy demeanor - he was full of jokes and kept me laughing until his accountant came to start their meeting. He came once a week for several weeks after that, each time with fresh stories that we all were now interested in hearing. His light personality was a welcome addition to the busy tax season traffic.

My penchant for unhealthy relationships had started taking a toll on me. My most recent boyfriend had decided to squat in my living room. No amount of arguing, tantrum-throwing, or going out with other guys was enough of a deterrent for him. Starving him out of my house backfired - he started pawning my CD collection and electronics. I called my leasing office only to discover that having him at my apartment was a lease violation and that we both would be evicted if I took action. I was dumbfounded that this guy had become so comfortable being unwanted and unliked.

One afternoon, Mike walked up to a hasty phone conversation, which ended with me slamming down the phone in anger.

"Woah, where's the smile?" he asked me.

"I hate men," I grumbled.

"Sounds like a pretty bad fight with the boyfriend," he replied with a coy smile.

"He's not my boyfriend," I snapped, "he's a leach who won't get off my couch."

Mike smiled an ornery grin. "Need me and my buddies to come handle it? I'm always up for a good brawl."

"I can fight my own battles, thanks."

The next day, Mike was back in the office.

"You don't have an appointment today," I reminded him.

"Nope. Hey, what do you do for fun?"

I cocked my eyebrow. "I go to concerts."

"Oh? Like who?"

"People you've never heard of," I challenged him. "I like Pat Green and Roger Creager–"

"Sweet! Cory Morrow is my favorite singer!" He got me there. Cory Morrow was Pat Green's college roommate and the guy who taught Pat how to play guitar.

"I sing." I was sure that one would turn him off. Men my age who listened to Red Dirt music were traditionally not fans of female singers. It was an inherent barrier to my career.

"Can you sing 'Maybe it was Memphis'?"

"Like, now?"

"No. Next time you're on stage."

"Fine," I said. "Tomorrow night is open mic night at the Pub. Buy me a beer and I'll sing your song."

The next night, Michael Knight was waiting at a table at the Pub with two Miller Lites and his infamous grin.

. . .

Eventually, Mike convinced me to change the locks on my apartment and head to a friend's house for the weekend. That fixed my couch surfer problem. Next, he convinced me to keep a standing Tuesday night happy hour date at a local Mexican restaurant. I obliged.

He wasn't my type at all. Michael Knight was smart, ambitious, energetic, and had laser focus. He was naturally flirtatious but rarely paid attention to the women who threw themselves at him. He worked from the first crack of daylight until it was completely dark, then, after a quick shower, threw on freshly starched jeans and a cowboy hat and was off to the clubs. He was an amazing dancer, and I am barely coordinated enough to walk downstairs without falling. Somehow, he was able to drag me onto a dance floor and swing me around to Charlie Daniels songs like I knew what I was doing. Spoiler alert: I still don't.

Our happy hour dates went something like this: meet at the bar, where Mike would be enjoying Round One, a cold Miller Lite. Eat free chips and salsa, with which Mike would order two Long Island Iced Teas. Order tacos, after which Mike finished his meal with a Jack and Coke. I usually nursed two to three beers in this time period, mostly because my stomach was too full of tortilla chips to fit anything else in it.

We talked about our jobs. We talked about my college classes, his business plans, and his parents' recent divorce. He was just easy to talk to, and he had made it clear that his intention for me was that he would be setting me up with his best friend, who was moving to town soon. I was fine with that idea - I had found a friend, and I trusted his judgment.

On one Tuesday evening, we started talking about relationship goals. Mike confided in me that he didn't take dating seriously because he was focused on building his business. He had spent his last year of college studying Jim McIngvale, a Houston furniture store owner notorious for his unique business model and philanthropic endeavors. "Mattress Mack", as he was called, had designed his business as a family plan, and credited his marriage with being one of the secrets to his success. Mike was searching for a partner, not a wife, and he wasn't going to settle for just anyone looking to simply be Mrs. Knight.

"What about you?" he asked me. "You planning on singing forever, or are you actually going to do this college thing?"

I shrugged. "I want to sing professionally," I confessed, "but I won't be hurt if it doesn't work out. I'd rather take the chance at it than wonder for the rest of my life if I could have done it."

"And college?"

"Backup plan," I answered. "I know I'm smart enough to do whatever I decide to do, I just want to make sure I'm ready if I change my mind."

"And marriage?"

I shrugged again. "I don't really think about it," I said. "I know some things that I don't want - like, I don't want to marry someone who doesn't have a life plan. It's OK to date them, but not marry. And I don't want to marry an alcoholic."

At that, Mike pushed away his Long Island Iced Tea and yelled at the bartender "water, please." The next Tuesday, we met at the bar, and Mike drank only Coke, no Jack.

By the next October, I was Mrs. Michael Knight.

My first year of marriage was awful. Not that Michael was awful - to his credit, his patience with me earned him sainthood. I became a stranger to both of us. Almost immediately, I began having dreams that Mike was killed in a car accident, died in his sleep, or just disappeared from the planet. I would wake up screaming and crying. I developed severe anxiety and a deep fear that I would be widowed at a young age. I would fight with him when he would leave the house to do anything except go to work. I would call incessantly when he was out with his friends, even locking him out of the house one night as punishment for sending me to voicemail. I had gone insane.

At the insistence of my husband, and because of my own exhaustion with my behavior, I agreed to seek counseling. Instantly, I was informed that I was a codependent. "You need Alanon," the therapist announced. I took her pamphlets home and studied up on this mysterious club.

I got angry. First of all, my dad wasn't drinking anymore, so why did I need a group for families of alcoholics? And second, his drinking was HIS problem, not MINE. Why did I need to join a club for crazy people who live with drunks when I wasn't even the problem here?

I attempted one meeting. I walked into a log clubhouse that had brochures lining every wall. I felt awkward. I casually perused the library. "One Day at a Time", "God, Grant Me the Serenity", "Codependent No More". This all sounded like hell.

"Are you here for a meeting?" a man's voice asked me. "AA is to the right, Alanon is to the left."

I felt humiliated. Does this guy think I could be an alcoholic?

"No thanks," I stammered, and I ran out the door.

I continued with therapy, but I refused to go to these awful meetings.

. . .

Mike and I had agreed to have three children. I was nearly done with my bachelor's degree and working full-time at another accounting firm when we decided that it was time to start a family. In my typical obsessive way, I began tracking, charting, spitting, peeing, and monitoring every other bodily function and fluid in an attempt to plan the perfect pregnancy.

A year into our attempts, I met with my OB/GYN. He explained to me that my previous emergency surgery may have left some scar tissue, and he wanted to do more tests. We agreed.

"The outcome isn't good," he said when he returned with the results. "Not only are your ovaries full of more cysts, but now there is severe scar tissue and uterine fibroids."

"So what does that mean?" I asked.

"Well," he said, "I don't give up too easily, but without some medical intervention, I'd say it's less than a 2% chance of pregnancy, even if we went straight to IVF."

In his standard easy-going style, Mike agreed that we would do whatever needed to come next. Even though the problem was with my body, he participated in every test, exam, and prodding that came his way. "It's OUR problem," he continually said. Still, I felt like a failure. Everything about his tests came out normal; my body, however, continued to show problem after problem. I underwent more surgeries with the hopes of making a comfortable nest for a baby. After a while, I gave up and enrolled in graduate school. If I couldn't be a mother, I'd focus on being an executive.

In December 2008, I graduated from college with my master's degree in accounting. I had set my sights on the advanced track and bypassed all other programs. Technically, I also have my bachelor's degree in accounting, but that was really a default degree for completing the MS program. I took the all-or-nothing approach to keep the fear fresh in me so that

I didn't quit. I focused my studies on taxes, oil accounting, and international business. My plan was to start with a large CPA firm, then move into the oil and gas industry. I was after the big money.

I loved my new career path. I landed a job at my first choice of an accounting firm, a large regional firm that was full of young, energetic people just like me. I was still helping Mike with his landscape business, but I finally had something that I could claim as my own career.

As I flourished, Michael became restless. He agreed that we were living a good life - two successful careers, weekends away from home, great relationships with our families - but, after he adapted to the idea of not filling our three-bedroom home with children, an unsettled energy came over him. One night, he confessed to me what was brewing inside of him.

"I regret not signing my ROTC contract," he said. "I was chasing the money, but I didn't chase the dream."

"OK, but it's a little too late now, right?" I asked. "I mean, you're 30 years old."

"Not really," he said. "I've already looked it up. I can still go into the Army, but I'm too old for officer school. And if I do it," he paused and took a serious tone, "I want to be commissioned."

I was careful with my next sentence. I wanted to support my husband, but I knew about the erratic nature of military life, and I wasn't prepared to live it again. "Is there any chance that you could become commissioned anyway?" I asked. I was sure that he would answer "no" and the conversation would be done.

"Yes," he said. "I could apply for an age waiver."

I sighed. "Are you going to do this?"

"Look," he said, still serious, "I've watched you do everything you have set out to do. For God's sake, you went from a run-down trailer to making six digits a year. I'll be honest - I'm jealous. You and your dad put your mind to doing something, and you do it. No fear. You don't even care if you fail, you just pull up your bootstraps and do it. I want to do that."

I hated to admit that he was right. Mike took the Knight way of approaching life - the safe way, the predictable way. He came from a family of attorneys, engineers, even senators. I couldn't deny him the experience of taking a risk, even a big one like enlisting. I was also swayed by my own family history - between my two parents, I had the honor of directly descending from a war veteran of each major war that the US had fought, even as patriots in the Revolutionary War. I bragged about it regularly. My generation was the first in the recent century to not have a military veteran, and I saw it as an obligation to at least be an Army wife.

The Alabama Experience

Michael took off to Fort Jackson, South Carolina for basic training. He was among the oldest in his class, but, in Mike's style, he remained the most competitive. Michael graduated at the top of his class, earning the physical fitness award. "And he would have won without the extra points for his age," the emcee bragged as Michael took his award. After being granted not one, but two waivers - his hearing was now shot after years of working on lawn mowers - Michael's mother and I saw him off to Fort Benning, Georgia, for officer candidate school.

My accounting firm had become a victim of the economy. The downsizing was now a regular occurrence. Being a top recruit, I had been repeatedly reassured that my position was secured and that I was on the partner track, but I didn't trust those promises. The laws of statistics were closing in on even the good accountants at my firm.

Mike and I decided to rent our house to a young couple and move to Fort Benning. Well, not exactly Fort Benning - my father convinced Mike not to live on base, but to find a house in the suburbs. We settled on Phenix City, Alabama. I hated it. I was in a new place with no friends, and I knew how isolated I would be while Michael completed training. I wanted to live on base, with the military community and other OCS wives. He wouldn't hear of it.

At the time, we had no idea how long we would be stationed in Fort Benning. His final career path was dependent upon his performance in officer school, and as determined as he was to continue being at the top of his class, he was being realistic about being a 31-year-old candidate. As such, I agreed to live in Phenix City.

I hated my job. I didn't make any friends, and I found it cumbersome to continue driving on and off base, given the heightened security measures and my work schedule. The upside was that my cousins were now living in Gulf Shores, so I could take weekends off and drive to spend time with family. They were my only social connection.

I hated my job so much that I found myself spending lunch hours in a local church. The Knights were a Catholic family, and my dad had married into a Catholic family, but I had no interest in exploring the faith myself. Still, I needed a meditation break, and the Catholic church across the street from my miserable job had mass at noon every day. I had no idea what was going on during that half-hour of bells and smells, but it was better than my gossip-ridden office or lonely living room.

The final field training wrapped up, and Mike came home ecstatic to report that he had finished in the top 10 of his class. "Infantry, baby!" he exclaimed.

"Wait. Infantry?" I knew that the fastest way to promote in the Army was as an infantry officer, but I also understood what this meant to us. Not only would we stay in Fort Benning for infantry and Ranger training, but my husband was going to spend most of his career on deployment.

"Yes! There are 5 open positions. I'm number 8 in my class!"

"But what if the top 5 take them first? What's your backup plan?"

"No backup plan," he said with a grin, "there are 3 women ahead of me."

Just as Mike was entering infantry training, my youngest brother enlisted into the infantry. It was great to have my family in Fort Benning to see him off, and Mike was excited that they would have this in common. My brother is 13 years our junior, so common ground wasn't easy for the boys to find. Mike was able to spend the weekend with him before he started basic training. Our family was officially an Army family now.

I was incredibly proud of Michael's achievements. I admired his courage for pursuing a military career at an age that was considered to be late in life, and I encouraged him to continue his training. At the same time, I resented his patriarchal decision to live in Phenix City. I needed a community in his absence, and I had been looking forward to living in Fort Benning. His decision came down to finances, and the fallacy that he and my dad believed that we made more money taking the housing allowance over the housing option. My voice in the discussion had been drowned out, even though I was the person who had to live with the decision day in and day out. While I was repeatedly invited to the base lunches, teas, and dinners, I rarely could make it to base on time to make the events. I was lonely, and I didn't feel like an officer's wife.

A condition of Mike's Ranger school approval was marriage counseling. The Army arranged for a therapist in Opelika and arranged his schedule so that we could make the appointments. The first appointment was very routine, with generic questions to each of us about our history, our families, and our relationship dynamics.

"You sound like business partners, not lovers," the counselor pointed out. We each looked blankly at her.

"But isn't that essentially what a marriage is?" Mike asked in his direct manner.

"Partly," she responded, "but it's also partly about love and romance. Debra, how do you feel about your romantic life?"

"I don't," I answered in the same direct manner. "I'm not a romantic kind of girl." Frankly, I was offended by her question. I had long ago become frustrated at the stereotype that I was supposed to be the romantic feeler in my relationships, just because I'm the girl.

We left, dissatisfied with our session, but committed to getting Mike into Ranger school.

Our next session was just as dry. In the end, the counselor reminded us that we required her signature before he would be approved for training. So, in the third session, I offered up my feelings as a sacrifice.

I shared my frustrations about living off base. I disclosed my disappointment in being an infertile woman, my disappointment in my career hiatus, and my fear of becoming a young widow. The topic of children brought me to tears. I was still grieving for the family that I would never have, for the emptiness that I was experiencing alone in that awful house.

At the end of the session, the counselor signed the paper that Mike needed to turn in to complete his Ranger packet. I was emotionally exhausted as I walked to the truck. Michael opened the door for me, but when I reached out for a hug, he shut the door in a haste.

We were halfway home when he finally turned to me and asked "so, wasn't that fun?" I looked at him in horror. He was smiling from ear to ear. I realized that anything he heard me say in that session was erased by his elation at getting his paper-work signed. "You sadistic son of a bitch," I thought to myself. I bit my lip and stared out of the window. He seemed oblivious to my pain.

Our lease was coming up for renewal. Since Mike was almost done with training and we understood the reality of immediate deployment, we decided that I would return to Houston. My brother had just completed his infantry training and would be deployed as well. It would be good for my entire family if we endured this together.

I decided that I would limit my resume submissions to oil and gas companies. I was selective in my applications. I had enough time to secure a job, and my current salary was so low that if I had to live without it for some time, we would still fare just fine.

I had also become more interested in the Catholic faith. My upbringing was very anti-Catholic, so my curiosity came as a surprise to me. I kept my studies quiet. I began attending a Catholics Come Home class in Columbus. I subscribed to Catholic Answers and started reading Scott Hahn's books. In the midst of this, I had my own spiritual awakenings that encouraged me to continue with this path. At the end of Lent, I called the Catholic church where Michael had been confirmed - where our home registration would be - and arranged to begin RCIA upon my return to Houston.

It was sometime during Lent when I received a curious phone call. "Hi, Debra? Hey, I came across your resume today. I'm a global consolidations manager and I have an open position. If I fly you to Houston on Friday, can you interview for my position?" Somewhere in the midst of that last sentence, I heard a young voice ask "Daddy, can we stop for fries?"

"Sorry," the voice said, "My daughter broke her toe and

we're on our way back from urgent care. Anyway, I'll pay for the flight and hotel."

I was impressed more that this man was taking his daughter to urgent care in the middle of a business day than I was about him calling me instead of pushing me off onto his HR team.

"Um, yeah, sure," I answered. "But my parents live just down the road from your office, so I don't need a hotel room."

"Oh, would you rather me fly you back on Sunday then? An extra day with the family on my expense report?"

"Sure!" I answered.

I spent that Friday interviewing and touring the office of a major oil and gas company, with this surprisingly friendly senior manager who was openly pro-family and very eager to hire me. My offer letter was twice the salary that I currently made, plus an amazing benefits package. I was elated. I was going to be an international accountant in the oil industry, and I was on my way home to Houston. Boxes - checked.

On family weekend, I filled Mike in about the job offer. He was excited. He had friends who worked at the same company and he knew what an opportunity this was for me. He was also very excited about the pay.

Then, I told him about RCIA. He was instantly disgusted.

"Where did that come from?" he demanded to know.

"I've been studying," I said excitedly. "I'm hooked! This is not at all what I thought it is. I love this church!" I expected him to become excited for me, but he only got more agitated.

"I feel like we should have talked about this first," he said.

My resentment kicked back in. I bit my tongue. Family weekend was not the time to argue about our faith, especially since it had been a topic we had agreed to nevver discuss from the beginning of our marriage. Still, I was surprised that he wasn't at least somewhat happy that I was coming around to his family's faith. I decided that it was too soon to make a big deal of the discussion, especially since I hadn't committed fully to joining the church.

Given how many changes were happening in my family, I decided to keep my marital issues to myself. I didn't even confide in my closest friends. Instead, I focused on moving back to Houston and starting my new job. I was excited to be home again and energized by this career change. My new position made me an insider for a publicly-traded company, which essentially just meant that I was limited to stock trading dates, but it looked great on a resume. Mike deployed almost immediately upon completing his training, so I was able to throw myself fully into learning about international accounting.

I was still angry with my body, though. It had betrayed me in my childhood, and now, it was stealing motherhood from me. I became obsessed with counting macros and heavy weight lifting, not to improve my body, but to chastise it. I spent weekends on long bike rides or running half marathons. I was not an athlete by any means, and this was the one area in my life where competition wasn't my goal. I was punishing my body.

My mother and I were estranged at this time. Shortly after I had left Missouri, my mother decided to become a corrections officer. I was proud of her for taking such a brave step. She was a small woman, barely five feet tall and still very small-framed, but that only made her even more determined to complete the academy. She was doing very well at her job when suddenly, she just abruptly left it. I had no idea that she had done this until a family member called me to ask why I was letting my mother move in with me. I was shocked. I learned that, after years of working at a maximum-security prison, my mother resigned and cut her lease short. She had her car packed and was on her way to Texas when I called to ask her what she thought she was doing. I refused to let her land at my house and instructed her to get back to the prison and get her job back. Instead, she headed to Gulf Shores.

With no mother to turn to for guidance, I leaned on Granny Wells. I decided to take a week to spend with her in Cedar Rapids. I needed someone to help me figure out how to navigate my marriage and heal my heart.

Granny did just the opposite. She lectured me on focusing too heavily on my education and career. She blamed me for not having children at a younger age and refused to acknowledge that I could just be infertile. "I had six babies, and your Grandma Nervie had ten. Dennis has seven children of his own. Don't give me this bullshit that you can't have kids - your cousins have never had an issue with it. You just don't want to be a wife."

There was never an acknowledgment from her that I was enough. I didn't have children, my marriage was failing, and I was the common denominator to both issues.

So many of my cousins have warm memories of Granny. She went to everyone's weddings but mine. It hurt to watch her hugging my cousins, and it still hurts when they share memories of her giving them advice and supporting them through the hardest times of their lives. It took me some time to figure out why she resented me so much - I was just like her. All of my grit, determination, and focus were the same that she had, except that I channeled mine differently than she did. It wasn't her fault. My grandmother grew up at a time when women didn't have careers, they had families. She worked until his last day to make her marriage to my alcoholic grandfather last, even through his neglect and public affairs. We really weren't that different. This realization became key to me. I made a decision that I would never again speak to anyone the way my grandmother spoke to me. It was the first act of self-recognition that I made.

Deployment wasn't as stressful as I imagined it would be. Communication was very different from what it was when my father was deployed. Mike would call or email every few days. He made it clear that he didn't want to get into the habit of daily communication so that I didn't panic when he was on assignment and couldn't be in touch. As such, I barely noticed when blackouts happened. I really only knew toward the end, when other wives would begin calling out of panic because they hadn't heard from their husbands. I didn't want to be the anxious wife.

I wasn't on base when Mike returned from Afghanistan. He didn't make a big deal of his return to me or his mother; as a matter of fact, he warned us that the dates would probably continue to change and recommended that we just stay home. Toward the end of his deployment, my company came under threat of a hostile takeover. Only a few insiders in the company were aware that this was happening, and we were put on call to respond to any immediate requests from the mergers & acquisitions attorneys. Meetings would take place at odd hours - noon on Saturday, 6 PM on Sunday - and we were required to have our laptops with us at all times. It was not uncommon to get a call on a Sunday morning to run financials without the tools division or wireline operations and email them to the SEC team immediately. The day of Mike's return was one of those high-energy days, and I wasn't even home from work until 1 AM. As nonchalant as he had been about his return home, he made sure to hold that day against me.

Mike had returned home just in time to be a part of my Easter confirmation. His base assignment was only 4 hours from our house, so the Saturday ceremony wouldn't be an impediment upon his schedule. I invited my aunt and uncle to come, too. My brother was also home from Afghanistan, and I asked him to be my confirmation sponsor.

The day was a big family celebration. We were all excited to have the boys home, and my stepmother was excited to see me joining her faith. My aunt and uncle were Baptist, and they were clueless about how big of a deal the day was to us, but they were happy to be a part of it.

Mike announced that afternoon that he wouldn't be coming to church with me. "I don't see the point," he said, "we're on our way to divorce anyway and this is basically lying to my church."

My heart sank. He had never used that word before. He had also been drinking all afternoon. I chalked the comment up to the alcohol and the stress of reacclimating to our large and chaotic family life.

The summer came with few visits from my husband. I offered to come to see him, but he refused. I didn't even have an address to where he lived. When he did come home, he spent most of his time drinking with his friends, ending the nights arguing with me about something I said or things I hadn't done correctly. When his mother and I approached him about the possibility of his mental health declining, he snapped at us "stop trying to ruin my career!" He made it clear that he was finally "happy" and that we were just obstacles to his success.

Physical safety has always been my personal boundary. Watching my mother repeatedly being abused by men, coupled with the sexual abuse I endured as a child, left me with a heightened awareness of my obligation to keep myself safe at all times. I had never feared Michael; quite the opposite, I saw him as my greatest defender. That soon changed.

Michael's late-night rants turned into physical altercations. Some nights, it was him dragging me out of bed to clean something; other nights, it was the demand to perform pushups as punishment for something I had said earlier in the day. I was too stubborn to entertain his crazy rants. I refused to even let him see how much they bothered me. He seemed to not remember the arguments the next day, and I decided that his drinking was to blame for the erratic behavior.

Our tenth wedding anniversary came, and Mike decided to take leave and come home for the occasion. I had hope that this meant a reconciliation. We chose our favorite restaurant for dinner - just a small place that was well known for its locally grown beef. Dinner came, and Mike was quiet. I tried reminiscing about the last decade of our life together. He grunted a few negative words. I choked back my tears. This marriage needed a hero, and I realized that I wasn't qualified to be that. At the end of dinner, he made a comment about this being our last anniversary together.

I chose to return to Missouri for Christmas. My aunt and uncle were starting to have health problems, and I wanted to spend the week with them and my brother, Roy. During our stay, Michael called me to let me know that he had just purchased a new truck for $55,000. I balked. I thought he was kidding.

"I deserve a damn truck," he barked into the telephone.

"But we haven't even discussed our budget!" I argued. "You're deploying again in the spring, can't you wait?"

"You never ask me if you can buy a purse, why should I ask you if I can get a truck?" And he ended the phone call.

I kept the conversation to myself. My family didn't need to know that my life was unraveling. Besides, I was certain that I could make a game plan to put a stop to this madness.

I returned home the next week to see the shiny blue

Chevrolet parked in our driveway. Inside the house, Mike was deep cleaning the house with loud music blaring - something he often did when he needed to decompress.

"Hey, I wasn't expecting you until tomorrow," he said in a shocked tone.

"I decided to drive straight through."

"Fine. I'll finish this and leave."

In a final attempt to reconcile, I said "You don't have to leave. I really appreciate everything you're working on here - I'll help. You can stay tonight."

He shook his head. "I don't want to," he said. "I have friends coming over to the cabin tomorrow." And within the hour, he was gone.

My 36th birthday came just a week after that conversation. I made a point to dress up that day. I curled my hair and wore my red lipstick. The compliments I received from coworkers helped to build my confidence, and, that night, I called Michael and told him that I would be filing for divorce.

Michael and I agreed to keep our divorce simple and low-key. He already had a list of what he wanted, so drafting the agreement was easy. It took only 61 days for the divorce to become final. Mike didn't come home for the hearing but sent his dad as his legal representative. He did come back the next week to help me and my father move my stuff from the house. He was in a great mood, even joking about our wedding album and who would take my dress. I was heartbroken that this was so easy for us to do after so many years of building a life together.

It didn't take long for Myron to learn that I was now a free agent. We had rekindled a friendship over the last few years, and Mike and I would sometimes visit with him when we came back to Missouri. He had divorced the same year that I had gotten married, and he was enjoying his life as a bachelor and a state trooper. I honestly took for granted that we would always just be platonic friends who happened to have been childhood sweethearts.

I was in the world alone, for the first time ever. I had gone from Myron, to my dad, to Michael. As tough as I appeared to be on the outside, I was terrified on the inside. Financially, I was in great shape; emotionally, I was a wreck. I feared dating again. I feared making any kind of decision again. I poured myself into my job and my friendships.

I was also making more trips back to Missouri. My mother had remarried, and, at the same time, she was beginning to show signs of ill health. My friends were starting to lose their parents, too. I was spending more time with my childhood friends and with my family, and, since he was also a part of my Missouri social circle, with Myron.

My company's hostile takeover attempt failed, but the exposure left them vulnerable to another buyout. Management was informed that our Houston office would endure a massive layoff as a part of the buyout package, and performance was not an indicator of who stayed. Instead, if the new parent company had a person in a duplicate position that our company had, it would be our employee who would receive the pink slip. In other words, their global consolidation team would prevail over our people, even if our people had a history of excellent performance. I decided to start looking for a house in Missouri.

Myron stepped up to help me in my house hunt. I would find a suitable property online, and he would drive to the location to investigate on my behalf. Everything was wrong in his reports back to me: a roof needed to be fixed, a yard didn't have good drainage, or a neighbor was a known felon that he didn't trust to live close to me. I was giving up on ever finding a house.

One afternoon, he called and laid his cards on the table.

"Here's the issue," he started in a matter-of-fact tone, "I know things. I know people and I have access to a lot of information."

I thought I was going to get another lecture about neighborhood safety. He continued with his speech.

"I'm picturing you living anywhere within a 100-mile radius of me, and I don't think that's going to work."

I was shocked. "We're friends, though. Do you think I'm going to cause some kind of drama?"

"No," he said, "but I will. I can just picture you trying to date, and I gotta tell ya, I'm going to make some ol' boy's life really uncomfortable."

I chuckled at this. "Myron, you're a grown man. I think you can handle it."

"Nope, I don't think so," he responded. "You see, you've always been the standard in my life. You're the one I compare everyone else to. It's easy when you're barely around, but now that I know you'll be here, it's just not going to work out well for either of us."

I still couldn't believe what he was saying to me. "What are you suggesting?" I finally asked.

"We just get married. Be done with it."

I laughed, hard. "Hey, Myron?" I asked. "Why don't you try asking me on a date before you propose marriage?"

A LEO WIFE

Frankly, I had no business being married again. I was wholly unaware of how emotionally unhealthy I was, and I was too proud to accept that I may have needed time to heal from the wounds of my first marriage. I can't remember what I was feeling; I don't think I ever allowed myself to feel anything. I knew that Myron was a safe person, and I honestly did love him as much as I was capable of loving another human being. I was just so accustomed to being numb that I had no idea how to feel again.

I remained on auto-pilot through wedding planning. We didn't have a long-term plan yet to get me back to Missouri, so we continued to live in separate states after the wedding. Myron had a young son from his first marriage, and the distance was a benefit to them as the family adjusted to this new dynamic.

A few months after our wedding, Myron reminded me that I needed to get serious about a job hunt. I tried companies in his small town, only to hear that I was overqualified. I tried companies in Springfield and was offered positions that included long-term non-compete agreements. I finally decided that St. Louis made the most sense. We agreed that I would look for an international accounting job in St. Louis, keep his farm in Texas County, and I would rent a small apartment in the city.

The plan worked beautifully. I interviewed for a position via Skype and was made an offer instantly. My start date was August 11, 2014. We leased a townhouse in St. Charles, and Myron came to Houston to move my things in advance of my relocation.

I left Texas on August 9, 2014. I arrived at the farm late that night to find Myron watching the news. A young black man had been shot by police in Ferguson, Missouri. I hadn't been to St. Louis since I was a kid, so I had no idea why this made my husband so nervous.

"They're talking about possible protests," he said. "You have to drive right through them to get to work. I'm moving my bride right into a hornet's nest."

I brushed off his anxiety. Myron always had high anxiety. Besides, our plan was that he would continue to be a rural trooper in Texas County. I would come to the farm on week-ends, and he would spend the weekdays that he had off work with me in St. Charles. I had no concerns that this would impact our lives in any fashion.

Later that month, Governor Nixon ceded the authority of Ferguson to the Missouri State Highway Patrol. State troopers were asked to volunteer to work riot control in the city, and Myron stepped up for the job. Our townhouse was only 15 miles from Ferguson, and he was certain that it would only be daily guarding of the local police station with a few responses to rowdy protestors. He saw the time as an opportunity for us to get our apartment in order and for me to experience life as a trooper's wife.

I didn't settle easily into St. Louis life. Houston is the kind of city that celebrates differences. There was a different cultural store or restaurant on nearly every block of town, and it wasn't unusual to meet someone who was a first or second-generation American. Montrose was known for its flamboyant clubs and parties that flaunted alternative lifestyles, and my friends and I loved spending Saturday nights in the district. In Houston, there doesn't seem to be a real minority, just different people.

St. Louis felt very different. Immediately, I was asked about my family name and what high school I attended. I didn't see how either of those facts were important. Where I lived also seemed to be a defining characteristic. It took me a very long time to understand that I was being sized up as "qualified"; for what, I still don't know.

One impactful conversation helped me to understand what kind of culture I had just joined. I was telling a story of my childhood, and an important detail to the point I was making was how we lived without electricity. Quickly, a female coworker shushed me.

"Don't say that out loud!" she said. I was surprised to hear her say this. She was a nice woman who seemed like a compassionate spirit.

"Don't say that I didn't have electricity? But I didn't," I told her.

"Maybe, but don't say it."

I was confused. "Why? I was poor - why is that a big deal?"

She lowered her voice to a whisper. "I grew up poor, too," she said, "but we don't say it. It makes people...uncomfortable."

"Uncomfortable? How? Why? They didn't take my money, we just didn't have it."

She shifted in her chair. "They don't like to hear about

that," she said, gesturing vaguely. "It's not something that we talk about here."

I was starting to understand the rules. We don't discuss race, we don't acknowledge poverty, and we certainly don't celebrate anyone who has overcome either of those two issues. But understanding the rules didn't mean that I agreed to play by them.

Overall, we were enjoying life as newlyweds. I loved coming back to Raymondville on the weekends and relaxing on our wrap-around porch in our country home. Myron loved date nights in the old part of St. Charles. We could be anonymous in the city, and keep our roots in the country.

Myron was also a helpless romantic. Before we got married, he gave me back the promise ring that he had saved every penny to buy when he was 16 years old. It was missing a diamond, but I had it handcrafted into a small wedding band so that I could wear it every day. He would also fill our apartment with roses or balloons, for no reason other than he wanted to. I wasn't used to this kind of attention, but it was growing on me.

Our family life was a little rocky, but nothing that I didn't expect. His son had never seen either of his parents in a serious relationship, even through all of Myron's single escapades. He was suddenly faced with accepting this new woman into his family and he had no idea how to digest it. I didn't let it bother me - Mason was just a kid, and a preteen at that. Myron was anxious about it, but I thought it was a benefit of keeping our farm in Raymondville. I had no issues with sitting out on certain weekends to let the boys have their own time. I felt that we had plenty of years ahead of us to acclimate to the new situation.

I drew the line on getting involved in the parenting dynamics between Myron and his ex-wife. I had seen how much trouble this had caused my father. It was hard to balance the "I stand by my husband" role with my "this is your child and you need to figure out how to co-parent" stance. My sympathies to anyone else who is experiencing this, because the truth is that you really do go through a long period of being in a no-win situation. If I had to give any advice, it would be this: mistakes will be made, just be careful not to repeat them.

November brought another call from the highway patrol for troopers to work in Ferguson. The grand jury hearing was scheduled to wrap up, and riots were rumored to be on the horizon regardless of the outcome. Myron chose to not answer the call this time. Even so, he was ordered to report for riot control.

I can still feel the angst of that week as our city sat on the edge of...something. We weren't sure what yet. The week is a blur to me. My husband left my house in full riot gear, and I didn't see him for several more days. At work, we kept our internet browsers tuned to the local news stations. Finally, someone yelled out "they didn't indict him!" The room was silent. One by one, we each grabbed our things and headed home - not because the workday was over, but because we weren't sure that we'd be able to get to our homes if we didn't leave right away.

I stayed plugged in all night. I couldn't have slept if I tried, so I just spent the entire night flipping between stations. At first, it seemed like an ordinary protest event. As the sun went down, I got myself into my pajamas and headed to bed - with the TV on.

Just as I started to drift off to sleep, I heard a report of gunshots. I bolted up in bed. No one knew who was shooting or where it was happening. I stayed alert. Next, my phone went off - someone was texting me to ask how Myron was, that they heard a trooper from his group was missing? I tried to blow it off as a rumor when the news reporter broadcasted "and now we have reports of a missing trooper. We're told that he's from Troop G - that's south Missouri, right?"

I cried. I grabbed a rosary from my nightstand and prayed. Hours went by. More gunshots. No news on the trooper. Suddenly, fires lit up my TV screen. Marked units were shown being turned over one by one, some with windows shattered.

"Firefighters are responding to a fire at Walgreens. Wait, we just heard reports that gunshots are heard from the Walgreens. Is that - are they shooting at the firefighters? Yes, the firefighters are now taking cover."

I went to the bathroom and threw up.

After another hour, a news reporter broke in with an update, "the missing G troop officer has been located and is reported to be safe."

Somehow, I managed to fall asleep for the next few hours, until I heard the click of the lock on my front door.

Myron was soaked from head to toe with sweat. I jumped up to hug him when he barked at me "Don't touch me! I've got tear gas from head to toe! Start the shower! And whatever you do, don't use the internet here." It was 6 AM.

When he got out of the shower, I asked about the missing trooper. It turns out that he was a classmate of ours, and the entire ordeal was because the guy had left his radio in his car and, when he turned around to get it, a group of rioters had taken over his unit. Unable to locate his men in the dark, he followed another group to safety.

Myron was exhausted, so I got dressed and went to work. Everyone's eyes were on me. I knew I looked a mess with my dark eyes and ratted hair thrown up in a messy ponytail, but I didn't care. They saw what I saw that night.

My director came to my desk to ask if I was OK. "I'm tired," I said.

"My neighbor is a trooper," she confided in me. "His wife stayed with us last night." She put her hand on my shoulder in a moment of compassion. "She woke up to a letter this morning telling her not to use her phone or internet. So be careful at home."

I had no idea what this sudden obsession was with our internet.

When I got home, Myron had our router unplugged and every shade in the house drawn. He explained to me that a group of people had been taking down badge numbers the day before, and had used the information to look up officer addresses. There were rumors that our phone and internet lines were being hacked. I don't know if that actually happened to us, but I did start finding social media pages dedicated to disclosing the photos, names, and work addresses of family members of officers who worked in Ferguson that week. No amount of reporting put a stop to the harassment. This was our new world.

It was the Ferguson drama that convinced Myron to leave Raymondville and move to the city. He was a true officer at heart, and rather than running from the battle, he wanted to fight in it. Even so, he was not experienced in city traffic stops nor the violence that came with city life. Rural patrol duty is dangerous but in a different way. I can't say that one is better than the other, they are just different, and they require a different level of training and experience. Myron decided to apply for a position as a highway patrol gaming officer for one of the five St. Louis casinos.

The idea was to get an "easy" position that would teach Myron more about fraud and white-collar investigations, something that he could use to start winding down his career with the highway patrol. The idea of wearing suits and driving an unmarked car appealed to him, especially since he was only 9 years away from retirement. He applied for an internship at Ameristar and was assigned to the Lumiere - the only casino in downtown St. Louis, just across the bridge from the notoriously dangerous East St. Louis.

Myron was told on his first day "don't buy expensive suits, you'll go through them quick around here." And he was shown an officer's jacket that was being sent to headquarters as evidence, one that had been sliced from neck to bottom with a switchblade. He was thrilled. Myron was still young enough to be in the fight.

He loved his new coworkers, too. Most of them were troopers who had been pulled off the road for excessive use of force, or for telling the brass to go to hell. They were the cowboys of the Missouri State Highway Patrol, with this one casino reporting more arrests than any zone in the state. The camaraderie was just his style. Myron was a cop's cop, the guy who jumped into the fight to save his own regardless of what was going down. He fit right in with this motley crew.

In August 2015, the news reported that a Harris County deputy was shot execution-style while fueling his car in full uniform. We were enraged. A protest was staged in Houston, and Myron demanded that I attend. I was happy to oblige.

I attended the pro-police protest with my stepmother and some of my Houston friends. It was peaceful with no counter-protests, and it was heartwarming to be back in an environment where people openly supported those who served. Coincidentally, I shared my flight home with one of Myron's coworkers, who was on her way back from a vacation with her husband. I thought the weekend was successful.

As I went to meet my connecting flight, I turned on my phone to find an unsettling voicemail from Myron. I called him back to hear him slurring over the phone in a frantic rage. "I could have killed him! I think I did kill him!" he kept shouting. I couldn't get him to calm down. I tried repeatedly and then, he hung up on me. I couldn't get him back on the phone.

Just before my flight took off, my phone rang. It was a coworker of Myron's. "I'm here with him," he assured me. "He's been drinking all night, but he's OK."

"What happened??" I demanded.

"We got into a fight last night. Some guy had a seizure just as we were arresting him."

"But who did he kill?"

"No one," his coworker answered, "He seems to think he kicked the guy in the head, but he didn't. I was there. I watched the footage. He never made contact. He took a step forward to put the cuffs on him when the guy went down in a seizure. Debra, the guy was overdosing on heroin. Myron had nothing to do with any of it. And I called the hospital - he survived."

I was so confused. "Why is he saying that he killed him?"

"I don't know," he replied. "But I've got his gun and I'm going to stay with him until you get home."

When I arrived home, Myron was asleep and his coworker was visibly exhausted. We were both confused about what had happened the night before, but we chalked it up to media overload and called it a day.

We decided to get as far away from the city as we reasonably could. We found a house just close enough for each of us to drive, but in a small community where we felt safe being ourselves. It turned out to be the dream house that we didn't know we wanted - a quaint four-bedroom, three-bath home on nearly four acres with a large shop for Myron's car hobby. I had my porches back, and the basement had a bedroom with no windows that were perfect for sleeping on the days when Myron had to work an overnight shift.

Mason was also struggling. He missed his dad, but he didn't want to leave his mom. His small school was becoming too overwhelming for him. He was a smart kid with anxiety issues - something he probably got from his dad. All of this led to a heated custody ordeal that could have ended traumatically for all of us but actually brought our family closer together. I developed a keen respect for Mason's mom, in spite of all of the fighting that she and Myron did. Mason came to live with us to attend high school. I was anxious about being a full-time step-mother, but he made it easy. He is a sweet kid with a keen wit and a loving spirit, and I was blessed to never have a power struggle or even any fight with him. My job was to make sure he stayed safe and healthy and to respect his parents and their rules for him.

The custody battle wreaked havoc on Myron's drinking. He would binge on his nights off work, turning into an unintelligible being with an overwhelming sadness. Four times, he tried Alcoholics Anonymous; four times, he came home telling me that he didn't feel safe at the meetings. I was becoming overwhelmed with his behavior. When he was sober, he was a loving, almost perfect partner. When he was drunk, he could barely stand up.

After his last failed attempt at AA, I had a mini nervous breakdown. I was at the end of my rope, and I had no idea what to do. I researched "how do I make my husband stop drinking?" and continued to get the result "attend Alanon meetings." I had blown this off 20 years before, but now the internet was telling me that Alanon had some secret that could make my husband stop drinking. On September 1, 2017, I stepped into my first recovery room.

I chose a noon meeting that was closed to only women. I walked in, found a chair in the corner, and sat quietly through the introduction. And then, I cried. The more the reader spoke, the more I sobbed. Each woman shared her most recent experience of enlightenment or story of recovery, and I cried harder. Random women would quietly touch my arm or my shoulder, and one mouthed to me "it's OK - we all cry our first time." I didn't understand why I was sobbing, and I'm not even sure if I got anything else out of that meeting, but I left feeling a huge release from my body. I continued to go back every Friday until the pandemic shut down all recovery meetings.

During this time, my mom had been battling stage three colorectal cancer. Her diagnosis brought us closer together. I spent many weekends in Springfield with her. One of my best friends was an oncology nurse, and I'd send her regular test results and letters for translation. Mom became a superstar on her chemotherapy floor, with nurses flocking around to hear her sing or tell a funny story. She had transformed from this bitter, crazy woman to a kind and warm cancer patient. I was honored to be witnessing this.

Aunt Louise and I sat with my mother during her last hospital stay. We spent those two weeks helping her make her final plans, giving her the strength to say "goodbye", and coordinating family visits. For the first and only time in my life, my mother and I prayed together. Even though she attended a Pentecostal church, my mother had a fascination with rosaries. I decided one day to teach her how to pray the Divine Mercy chaplet on her rosary, a prayer that Catholics often recite on behalf of the dying. Until her last breath, my mother continued to chant the words from the Divine Mercy photo that I gifted to her, "Jesus, I trust in you".

My mother died in December 2017. We had her funeral in Texas County, and dozens of uniformed officers who had never met my mother made a presence at her visitation. "This is what we do," Myron whispered to me. "You're now a part of a family that will always show up for the hard stuff."

That Christmas, Myron started experiencing severe migraines. The pain was so severe that his sergeant sent him to urgent care for a spinal tap. The results came back inconclusive. He continued to be plagued over the next week, howling during the day because the light hurt his eyes, and sobbing at night because he couldn't sleep. I took him to the emergency room. Some poor man whose wife was having a heart attack stopped and prayed over us. A man who was holding his cut-off ear in a towel offered him condolences. His misery was intense, and we all felt helpless.

To make matters worse, Myron had started breaking out in a mysterious, painful rash. The rash seemed to coincide with his pain. Blood levels showed elevated ANA values and high cortisol rates, but he had no official diagnosis. He became unable to sleep, and the less he could sleep, the more he drank. The vicious cycle left him utterly useless.

On January 21, 2018, Myron took Mason shopping for an upcoming dance. In the middle of the store, Myron fell down in a full seizure. He was rushed to the hospital via ambulance. I arrived to find a room of state troopers, working to keep his spirits up, but whispering uneasily to one another.

"Where am I?" Myron asked.

"You're in the hospital," I replied.

"What day is it?"

"Sunday."

"What happened?"

"You had a seizure."

"Well, that's a career killer." And he fell asleep.

Five minutes later, Myron woke up and looked at me.

"Where am I?" he asked.

"You're in the hospital," I replied with agitation.

"What day is it?"

I sighed. "It's still Sunday."

"What happened?"

"You had a seizure."

"Well, that's a career killer." We repeated this conversation at least half a dozen times before Mason ordered me to just stop answering him.

Myron was in the hospital for three days before being released. He had no diagnosis and was put on six months of medical leave. To kill time, he grew a beard and took on a daily hobby of drinking. The upside to his hospital stay was that the rash mystery was solved. Myron had been diagnosed with psoriatic arthritis, and the doctor's theory was that it was brought on by his constantly elevated adrenal levels.

By this time, I had changed jobs and was working for a large Catholic charity that specializes in poverty services. Working with social workers was a huge shift for me, but the compassion that they gave me through the chaos of the year was exactly what I needed. I also found a means of sharing my childhood story. Many people were fascinated to hear how I came from poverty to a successful finance career, and I was grateful to be giving back to my community.

Myron, on the other hand, was falling apart. I was often awakened to hearing him reliving stories in his sleep - some were car accidents, others were line of duty deaths. All were in great detail, and he would bolt awake with beads of sweat pouring from his face. All that I could do was hold his hand or touch his face, speaking gently to remind him that he was safe at home with me. Some nights ended in tears. Other nights, he would put his jeans on and confine himself to his shop with a pack of beer.

I began researching some of the incidents that I suspected were haunting Myron. He kept scrapbooks of news stories and letters, so it was easy to do. Sometimes, he would wake up yelling "get his legs out of the road!" - I learned that this story was directly correlated to a traffic stop where his friend and coworker was run over by a speeding car. Other nights, he would scream "someone get the dog out of the truck!" I found a news story of a truck driver who was trapped in his truck with his dog as they burned alive, and Myron was the officer in charge of the investigation. There were stories of drowned babies and teenagers killed in car accidents, all of which I had learned about in his sleep.

I started finding handguns in his shop. Myron was an avid gun collector, but I knew that most of these weapons were traditionally locked in a gun safe. Random bullets would roll out from under the shop furniture. Soon, the guns were within arms reach of him. He acted like nothing was wrong, but I was starting to freak out.

One evening, I called the boys to the table for dinner. Mason sat down, and Myron said he was going to the restroom to wash his hands. Several minutes went by without Myron.

"I think you should check on Dad," Mason said. "He might have gotten sick."

I knocked on the bathroom door. There was no answer. I said his name, and still, no answer. Worried that he may have had another seizure, I opened the door. Myron was sitting fully dressed on the commode with a gun in his mouth and tears streaming down his face.

"What are you doing?" he yelled at me. "You aren't supposed to see this!"

I was frozen. "Dinner is ready" is all that I could say.

"I'll be there in a few minutes."

In a zombie-like trance, I went back to the table and sat down. Myron followed just moments later.

"Sorry son," he said casually, "I guess my stomach is upset today."

I knew better than to ask for help. I had confided once in his sergeant when the nightmares began, and Myron had come unglued. I wasn't scared of what he would do to me, I was scared of what he would do to himself. I also believed that I was the only person who was dealing with this level of chaos. No one had ever talked to me about officer stress, and I had never heard of police suicide before. We just didn't talk about it.

I decided to use my Alanon tools to deal with his mental health issues. I made the conscious decision to love my husband through his ordeal, rather than lecture him or get angry at his drinking. When he struggled, I let him cry on my shoulder. When he drank, I left him alone.

One night in May, Myron confided in me that he was disgusted with his alcoholism. "I want to stop," he said, "but I've got stuff."

I found the courage to say to him "then let's deal with the stuff before we worry about the drinking."

"What do you mean?" He seemed shocked that I made reference to "the stuff". I was scared to say what came next, but I did it anyway.

"Have you ever thought that you may have post-traumatic stress disorder?" I heard him let out a huge sigh, and then, silence.

"Why do you think that?" he finally asked.

So I told him. I repeated to him the dreams I heard him have, the details that he would say in his sleep. I told him about how he would lose track of where he was and reminded him that I had to talk him out of those trances to bring him back to me.

"Can you leave me alone for a while?" he asked. I was scared of what he may do next, but I respected his wishes.

After about half an hour, Myron found me. "I think you're right. Let's get help - just don't let the patrol know." And so, I set out to find help for Myron.

In June 2018, we were off to participate in an anonymous suicide prevention study in Utah. It was funded by the Veterans Administration, but we were among the first group of officers for which data was being gathered for a federal grant. For the first time, each one of us found people just like us. He found officers and veterans that were big, tough guys, who regularly fought the urge to swallow a bullet. I found wives who were also dealing with nightmares and the angst of addiction and suicide attempts.

The cognitive-behavioral therapy that Myron received made a strong impact on him, but he still wasn't ready to give up the drinking. He had convinced himself that he could wean himself from his now case-a-day habit, but we all knew that this wasn't going to happen. Another month went by like this, until one night, I found him on the back porch with his duty weapon in hand, his badge on his chest, and a note on the table that read "I'm sorry sweetheart. I tried."

"I'm going to the woods to do it," he said in almost an apologetic manner. "Don't let my guys find me. Call county, but don't call my guys until they find me."

I sighed and sat down. "You know what, Myron?" I said in an exhausted tone, "I give up. I realize that I cannot stop you from shooting yourself if you're this determined to get the job done. So, know that I love you and I wanted something better for you, but I can't fight your demons anymore."

Myron sat down and stared at me. "Like that? You just give up, like that?"

"It's out of my control," I replied. "One of these days, I'm going to go to work and you're going to finish the job. I can't sit here with you every minute and stop you. I don't want you to die, but you seem to want it more."

He put the gun down. "I'm sorry," he said. And he cried. When he was done, we went to bed.

The next day, on my way home, Myron called me screaming. I couldn't make out what he was saying, and eventually, I hung up the phone. He called back. "GET ME HELP!" he screamed into the phone. "JUST GET ME TO A HOSPITAL."

I came home to find over 30 empty beer cans on the back porch, and two guns in front of Myron. "Take me to the hospital and put me on a 96." A 96 referred to the 4-day mental health hold that was generally involuntary after a person tried to commit suicide.

"Let me get the car," I said.

"No," he argued, "call the county. I want the county to take me in so that I can't check myself out."

"Myron, that's going to get back to your lieutenant..."

"Fuck them," he said. "It's time they know what they've done."

I called the number to dispatch and explained that my husband, a state trooper, was threatening to kill himself and I needed a car and that he was voluntarily going to the hospital. The dispatcher responded to me "Let me give you another number to call. That line isn't recorded, and you can give me his name and address. I'll call the sheriff directly." And so, we arranged for the sheriff and two deputies to come pick up my husband.

I went downstairs and informed Myron of the process. And then, I demanded that he explain to his son what was happening. I was supportive of his decision, but I wasn't going to clean up his mess.

Mason took the news better than I had expected. He had just lost two classmates to suicide, so the threat of his dad's own death was real. He hugged his dad, reassured him that we would support him through this, and sat with us until the squad cars arrived. We watched as they patted my husband down and cuffed him ("Procedure, just for safety" they explained while Myron nodded to us), and then, we watched them drive away with my husband. We cried together, cleaned up the beer cans, and emptied the rest of the alcohol that we could find in the house.

Early the next morning, my phone rang. It was Myron's new sergeant, who was on his way to my house to get Myron's duty weapons. At 6 AM, two troopers walked into my house and sat at my table.

"His blood alcohol content was .40," the first trooper reported. "He should be dead."

"He keeps trying," I replied.

"We find that these matters generally reflect an uneasy home life," the second trooper informed me. "What exactly is going on here that we need to know about?"

I felt my head explode at that moment. "You want to know what's going on?" I retorted. "I'll tell you what's going on. My husband's body is falling apart, and none of you ever call to check on him or come by to see if he's OK. He gave you his all in Ferguson and you keep telling him to keep his mouth shut about it, while Ron Johnson is all over Amazon for his book about being a black officer in St. Louis - but you don't stop him from selling his guys out. No one has ever helped me learn how to deal with my husband's nightmares or cold sweats, but you get pissed off that he's drinking himself to death. And then you come into MY kitchen and accuse ME of being the problem?" I found myself poking #2 in the chest now. "Listen," I continued, "I'm the toughest son of a bitch in this room. When you find yourself hiding behind a quarter panel because bullets are flying by your head, you know if you're safe. I only see on Twitter that someone saw your car there. When you are in the middle of a fucking riot, you know if you're the guy who's missing. I am stuck following the news story. When you are responding to shots fired, I'm here making sure a kid is getting his homework done and trying to keep the house normal so that he has no idea that his dad might be the guy who just got his head blown off. I know how to keep a fucking normal house. And I'm the one who is here every goddamn night coaxing that Glock out of my husband's mouth while you fuckers sit around judging him for falling apart."

The first officer stood up and gathered the weapons from the table. "Ma'am, I think we should go now."

"You bet your ass you'd better go", I hissed.

"We'll arrange for someone to get whatever we've forgotten. And our lieutenant will probably be calling later."

"He fucking better." And I slammed the door behind them.

Four days later, I picked Myron up from the hospital. We hadn't been allowed to visit him. Every time we tried, the one visiting hour he was allowed to have had been changed. I was relieved to finally get my arms around his neck.

Myron sat in my car and took a deep breath. "I guess it's decision time - do I want to go get a beer, or do I want to go home?"

I didn't say anything back; I just said a silent prayer to myself.

"I think I want to go home," he finally said. "Let's try this without the drinking for a while."

Recovery was difficult, but it was beautiful. Myron filled his days in the shop and spent his nights reading his Bible. He went to a church retreat and found strength in the stories of men who were so much like him. Doctors had put him on sleeping medication, and he was working to keep the same hours that Mason and I kept so that he could enjoy family time with us at night.

About a month into his recovery, I got a call that an officer that Myron worked within Texas County was found in his living room by his daughter, dead from a self-inflicted gunshot wound. The officer who called me wanted to know if anyone was with Myron because his friends were now scared that this death would trigger him.

Myron took the news surprisingly well. He went to the funeral and shared his own story of his struggles with his friends. It was the first time that he had openly admitted to being suicidal. We received an outpouring of support, and Myron felt empowered by the ordeal. He came home and committed to serving officers struggling with suicide - he just needed more time to work on his recovery.

On his bad days, Myron would go to the calendar and count days, and this made me anxious the first several times that he did it, but I learned to let him handle his recovery in his way over time. He was seeing a therapist weekly and a psychiatrist monthly. The house was clean again, and he found hobbies to complete while we were at school and work. He also started taking classes to become a certified trainer. He was already a firearms instructor, but Myron wanted to expand those skills to training on mental health and dealing with the stress of the job. However, he knew that the writing was on the wall - he was soon going to run out of medical leave and would be forced into medical retirement. He seemed fine with this idea; he just needed an avenue to keep him connected to his community.

During this period of self-discovery, Myron started researching other former officers who trained law enforcement officers in mental health. He was finding inspiration in their stories. He found one couple in Texas who called themselves That Peer Support Couple and made me watch a video with him that told their story. Javier and Cathy Bustos were both former law enforcement officers who were now dedicated to helping other officers with trauma incurred on the job. Myron was inspired. He asked me to reach out to them, but I never did. I needed to first know that he was better before I threw him back into the fire.

Myron had the idea that he and I would train people together. He had planned on sharing his story and let me tell mine from a spouse's perspective. He was a gifted speaker, and I had no doubt that he would be influential in his testimony. Mine, however, seemed incidental. I wasn't confident that anyone would want to hear about sleepless nights and long days incurred by a tired law enforcement wife. Still, I held on to the idea.

In April 2019, Myron received his final separation packet. He also relapsed.

The drinking came on quickly one day. He called me while I was at dog training to tell me he couldn't make it. He was in his Jeep at a bar, and he was drunk. After nine months of peace and joy, our chaos was back.

To his credit, Myron did try to control the volume of his

drinking. He had even confessed his relapse to his counselor - though I learned later that he told her that Mason and I were alright with it. We were not.

By July, he was back to a full case a day, but this time, he brought rage into the picture. His suicide threats had become an every night ordeal, with some nights involving him waking me up to see a gun to his head and him begging me to stop him. I stopped sleeping, and I could barely eat. I had become rail-thin. People accused me of dieting, but the truth was, I was barely functioning. My head hurt all of the time, and I was scared to go home at night for fear of finding him dead.

One night, he sat me down and informed me that he was having outrageous thoughts. He wouldn't go into detail, and I couldn't imagine what could be more outrageous than suicidal ideations.

"Just promise me that you won't let me hurt you or Mason. You promise?"

I blew him off. "You're a threat to yourself, Myron. You've never hurt us; I can't imagine that you ever would."

Myron grabbed my arms and shook me. "Promise me! Don't let me hurt my son! And kill me if I ever hurt you. I need to hear you say that you promise me this!"

For the first time in my life, I was scared of Myron. "OK," I agreed. "I promise."

"Hold me accountable like you would anyone else."

"OK, I will. I will!"

And with that, he let me go.

On November 15, 2019, I woke up to hear glass shattering in my garage. I had no idea what could be happening. I stumbled out of the garage door to see my husband's Jeep Wrangler ramming into the side of my house. At first, I thought he had gotten drunk and lost control of his vehicle. When he put the Jeep into reverse and then drove back into the garage, I realized that he meant to do exactly what he was doing.

The 911 call lasted 23 minutes. It was a full 23 minutes of Myron running into my house, coming inside to drag me outside, calling me names the entire time, and blaming me for his uncontrollable behavior. I kept the operator on the phone but hid the phone from Myron when he would come back inside to drag me out.

My only thought was how to keep Mason from seeing this nightmare as it unfolded. I had two reasons: first, Mason was now 18, and I knew that he would think he was big and strong enough to physically stop his father - a decision that could kill him. Second, I just didn't want Mason to see his father like this. He would see the aftermath soon enough, but he didn't need to witness the violence firsthand.

Guns were soon involved. Myron waved a gun at the dogs, threatening to shoot them. He waved a gun at me. He put the gun to his head, then dropped it and went back outside to finish the job that he was doing in the Jeep. I worked to keep his focus on the south side of the house since Mason's room was on the north side. It felt like the cops were never going to get to the house.

Soon enough, Myron was aiming toward Mason's room. I dragged Mason out of bed and ordered him to put his shoes on and follow me to the basement. We each grabbed the dogs and ran for the shop, which, fortunately, was unlocked. I locked the door behind us and we waited there until I could see the lights of the squad cars.

"Get out of the car," a loudspeaker yelled. "Sir, put down your weapon. I SAID PUT THE GUN DOWN! Now, get your hands above your head."

I hated that my stepson was hearing this. He was barely

awake enough to be walking, much less understand what was happening. Then, a loud bang came from the shop door. "Mrs. Downey!" a voice yelled. "Mrs. Downey, this is the sheriff's department. We have your husband in custody and I need you to open the door."

A group of deputies escorted Mason and me back to the house and sat us down at the kitchen table. They took statements, though Mason refused to put his on record. An officer approached us and informed us that Myron was in the car ranting things such as "just put a bullet in my head now" and "please, just let me die."

"He's suicidal," Mason said flatly. "He absolutely means it."

Another officer looked at me. "Is that true?"

"Yes," I replied, "that's why he did this. He's been trying to die for almost two years."

I could see the light bulbs go off. "We're going to put him on a 96 - that will buy time to get a judge to sign the warrant. Ma'am," he looked at me directly now, "We're charging your husband with first-degree domestic assault, and I'm asking for a cash-only bond. Do you know what that means?"

I didn't understand anything anymore.

"That means that this is out of your hands. I don't want you bailing him out, and if he's found guilty, there will be a default permanent restraining order on your husband."

Another officer interjected by handing me a folded piece of paper. "This is the number to victim services," he said. "I recommend filing for a temporary restraining order first thing in the morning. We have no control over when the hospital lets him go, we can only hope they call us first."

A group of firefighters appeared from my basement. I had no idea they were even there.

"The electrical is fine - they can sleep here tonight. But

those walls - " he pointed to the massive holes in the side of my living room " - they need to be covered before the temperature drops any further."

Another group of firefighters went to work shielding my home from the cold with large sheets of plastic.

The officer who had given me the paper began inspecting my arms. "Did he put those bruises on you?" he asked.

I looked at my arms. "No, I just get bruises," I replied.

"What about that cut on your finger?"

I looked down. I had no idea that I was even bleeding. "I probably got that in the shop," I said. "He's never laid a hand on me. I don't even know where this all came from."

The officer looked at Mason, and Mason nodded. "He's not violent, just a drunk asshole," Mason confirmed.

Soon, everyone left, and we stumbled off to bed. I woke up the next morning to inspect the final damage. The garage was a total loss. My car and his motorcycle were buried under a pile of rubble. The Jeep was still in the front yard, with the grill guard full of mortar from the brick that was in piles, and the fenders were severely beaten. There was no exterior wall left in the office. The glass on my front door was shattered. My front yard looked like a tornado had hit my house - a perfect picture of what had become our lives.

I took Mason's car to the courthouse and met with the victim services advocate. From there, we filed for a temporary restraining order. Mason's mom convinced him to do so as well, to set a clear boundary for his father and to protect everyone around him. My phone began ringing - the highway patrol had been called by the sheriff's department. Soon, my yard was full of state troopers and trucks. They cleaned up as much of Myron's mess as they could, and then, they arranged a series of safe houses for me to stay in until Myron was finally arrested. Mason would go to his mother's house. None of this was an official order; these were our friends, and they were genuinely scared for my family.

Myron did come back. Once he was released from the hospital, he walked the 9 miles to our house with the restraining orders in hand. My neighbor saw him on our road and called me at work to let me know that he was coming, and he looked pissed. What Myron didn't know was that my dad was holding fort at my house. He had repaired the security cameras and watched as my husband knocked on windows, tested doors, and finally broke into our shop. He could see Myron reach above the doorway for the shotgun that we normally kept there (another clue that he was out of his mind - he knew I'm smart enough to remove all firearms from anywhere he could have gotten them).

My father was waiting for Myron at the back door with his gun. Upon seeing him, Myron fled to the woods. Both my father and I were on the phone with 911 - me from my car, him from my basement. No one seemed in a hurry to get to my house, it didn't even seem that they could see the assault charges or restraining orders in their system. Finally, I hung up and called the highway patrol.

"This is your problem," I told his lieutenant. "He is your guy, you trained him, and we need your help finding him before he kills someone!"

They offered to bring dogs. I told him that it would probably be a good idea.

Less than an hour later, Myron was in custody. I'm told that he found a payphone at a gas station and reported that my father was at our house, threatening to kill him. He was apprehended and denied his request for a personal recognizance bond - the judge supported the arresting officer's recommendation for a cash-only bond. My husband was taken to the county jail and, after numerous change requests on his behalf, our court date was set for late March 2020.

I used the time alone to focus on my recovery. Instead of running away, I ran to find myself. I ran to Alanon meetings, I ran to women's retreats, and I ran to my church's women's group. I realized early on that I had a choice: I could fight the state and spend all of my energy scraping together the money to bail my husband out of his own problems, or I could heal in solitude. I thought back to the many friends I had over my lifetime who had stories of abusive friends and family members, who confided in me how much of a betrayal they felt when a parent in their lives chose their abuser over their safety. I remembered back to my mother's own pattern of falling into one abusive relationship after the next. I remembered my husband's personal boundaries, and how he kept his own childhood abusers far from us, regardless of their blood relationship, in an attempt to break the pattern for his son. I chose to heal.

I began a daily routine of meditation, prayer, and reading. I stopped working late hours. I leaned into my support system, which included mine and Mason's families. We were blessed to be engulfed in so much love. As a family, we made a recovery plan. We found resources for Myron that included in-patient treatment and gave the information to the prosecuting attorney and to the people in our circle who stayed in touch with him. We agreed to leave the rest of his recovery in God's hands and to focus the rest of our energy on our own mental health.

My road to recovery had to start with loving myself. I hated running, so I stopped doing it. I added red meat and carbs back to my diet and started hiking because these are things that I enjoy. I packed my scale and allowed my jeans to go up one size.

I was done punishing my body for things that were out of my control.

I forgave myself. I forgave the women who had come before me. I stopped looking for our flaws and started realizing how strong we were. I had focused so much attention on how many of Granny Wells's toxic traits that I had inherited that I failed to recognize how much grit and determination she must have had. I was angry that I couldn't be more like Grandma Nervie, with her sweet and soft disposition. I realized that I was equally made up of both women, and I chose which of each one's traits I wanted to embrace. I could be kind and tough. I didn't need to be one or the other. I could dig my heels in the way my mother would when she focused on a goal, and not have to default to her codependent behavior when I became scared.

I redecorated my house. I bought the couch that I had wanted for years, the one that Myron argued against because he hated sectionals. I redid the floors and the window treatments. When the time came to put together the office that he had driven through, I chose a soft, feminine theme for my workspace. I changed our bedding and created a space where I could sleep again, comfortably, without resentment or anxiety.

The office was the last part of our home that I was able to tackle. Myron had literally driven through the space on the night of his attack, taking out the wall and leaving behind the wreckage of furniture, papers, and pictures. Sorting through our bills was emotionally exhausting enough for me, but my resentment and grief were further escalated when I uncovered the binders that documented the work Myron had been doing during his moments of lucidity.

He had compiled documents of research focused on the impact of repeated trauma on first responders. There were worksheets that walked through how to apply cognitive processing tools to subjects suffering from post-traumatic stress reactions. Myron had put together a presentation focused on the OODA loop and its effectiveness in law enforcement; the presentation was marked with positive feedback from a training instructor who encouraged him to share his work within the law enforcement community. The biggest gut-punch was notebooks with brainstorms of ideas for what he planned to do with this information. He had lists of organizations to call, people to email, and detailed plans on what to discuss in his presentations. He wrote plans for me, too - plans to share how post-traumatic stress disorder impacted our marriage and family, ideas about articles for me to write that shared my testimony. The business names that he brainstormed indicated that he was determined for us to do this as a couple.

It saddened me to see this work wasted. I still felt strongly that Myron could turn his life around and use his mental breakdown to warn others against self-medicating their problems. I just knew that it wouldn't be likely that we would ever do that work together. Soul searching led me to accept that I wasn't sure if I would ever trust my husband again to not relapse and repeat his violent behavior. Still, I had no intentions of divorce; I was praying for a miracle.

The Covid pandemic put off our March trial date. We would not have a hearing until August 2020. With each day that passed, I grew more anxious. I worried about his safety as a LEO in a county jail. I was told by someone that he was in solitary confinement for his safety; that worried me more. Myron did not fare well in isolation. As we neared the trial, I carefully worked out a recovery proposal and shared it with the prosecuting attorney. Myron was on my health insurance, and I would keep him on it for as long as he was in recovery. I identified three law enforcement-friendly mental health hospitals that specialized in dual diagnosis. I had no idea how we would pay for any of this, but I made it clear that I wasn't worried about the money. Whether he ever came home or not, I wanted Myron to recover.

The week of the trial, Myron's attorney called me to outline their plan. Myron would return to Texas County to live with a friend, someone that I was informed had power of attorney over his finances and health. When I expressed concern about this, he said to me "You need to file for divorce. That will make everything marital property, and it's the only way to keep you protected. Besides," he continued, "once we make our plea agreement, the judge will put a permanent 'no contact' order on Myron. He will never legally be able to see you again."

"I need your help to get him to recovery before he kills himself," I pleaded.

"If he wanted to kill himself," his attorney responded, "he would have done it already. These guys know how to do it when they want it done. Just take care of what you need to do."

The idea of the state being able to take my family away without my consent made me sick, but I understood the intention. The state had put strict domestic violence laws together that were designed to keep us safe from our attackers. I was angry with Myron for choosing this road, and even angrier when a strange IPO began to log into our online banking systems and attempt to move money from our accounts - MY accounts. Myron hadn't worked in over a year, and any money that we had was from my salary. It was like I was being physically attacked all over again.

I refused to make a statement at Myron's hearing. I had nothing to say. He knew what he had done, and I wasn't going to give him fuel to react in any way. After the hearing, I met with a divorce attorney. I asked to file for separation; she enlightened me to the inner workings of our civil court system and advised that, if I wanted a judge to take me seriously, I should file for divorce with the caveat that I would drop all proceedings when Myron accepted our offer for treatment. I expressed my concerns that he would move forward with his plan to kill himself; she reiterated the sentiments of his attorney, adding her observation that these tended to be empty threats used by abusers to control family members.

Myron was continuing to get messages to me. One day, I would be told that he wanted me to file for the divorce, that he agreed to give me everything and just wanted his life back. The next day, another friend or family member would reach out to me expressing Myron's regret over his actions, reassuring me that he promised to do anything he needed to do to get his family back. To both messages, I responded with the treatment center information. I wasn't going to be emotionally manipulated either way.

While he was ordered to remain far from us, I knew that he had been coming back to our town. Neighbors and friends would report seeing him, saying that he explained his presence by citing doctors visits or business to be handled. I came to understand that my life going forward would be a constant motion of looking over my shoulder and wondering if he was going to come back with even more of a vengeance. I just kept giving my anxiety to God.

On the morning of September 29, 2020, I woke up to my normal routine of morning coffee and prayer. As I sat to read scripture and begin my rosary, I realized that the date signified the Feast of the Archangels - a day that, historically, Myron and I would gather to say a prayer of protection to St. Michael the Archangel. My devotion to this day remained strong, but I was tired and angry. I was tired of Myron continuing to deny his accountability in the mess that had become our lives; I was angry that I felt forced to file for divorce in an attempt to save myself. I wanted my dream back, I wanted him to want help, and I wanted to know that his family was important enough for him to choose recovery.

In the midst of my anger that morning, I felt an overwhelming reminder to pray for Myron anyway. He was still my husband, I still loved him very much, and, even if he chose to become my enemy, we are taught to pray for our enemies. As such, I expressed my prayer intentions out loud. "Lord, I dedicate this rosary to Myron and I pray for the miracle of recovery, for him and for our entire family. Even so, let your will be done." And I completed my rosary with a prayer to St. Michael.

I left work that morning for a doctor's appointment, one that required me to fast and not drink water for several hours before testing. The tests were scheduled to take 2-3 hours, and we were halfway through them when the doctor suggested a blood draw to be added to the scans. I knew this would be problematic - I have always struggled to give enough blood, and I knew my body well enough to know that I required a lot of hydration to make this a success. The staff came up with a plan to lay me down, give me juice, and hook me to an IV. We would wait in a low-lit room until noon when the doctor would need to move on to the next test.

As I had warned the staff, we waited for a long, long time. I didn't feel nauseous or faint, I just felt...bored. Eventually, I closed my eyes to try to relax and let the juice rehydrate my body. I suddenly felt jerked back to my house. I was on my back porch, sitting with a friend when I had a panicked urge to walk to the other side of the house and up the driveway. There stood Myron. I was incredibly lucid - I asked myself "why am I in my driveway if I'm at the hospital?" And then I yelled at Myron "why are you here? You have a restraining order, you aren't supposed to be here!"

But he kept coming down the driveway. He looked as

though he had just come in from a rainstorm, but it was a clear, sunny day. He was staggering, his face sunken in, and he just kept walking toward me. I panicked. I started to turn and run when a loud voice came over me. "Grab him!" the voice yelled. It was the same voice that I had heard when I was a little girl in church. I started to argue when I heard "just shut up and grab him!" And so, I let Myron fall into my arms. We fell to the driveway together, and he began to sob. He held onto my arms, and I felt such peace overcome me as I stroked his hair. "It's OK," I reassured him. "You're home now. It's OK."

And then, my eyes opened with a startle. The nurse quickly responded. "Are you ok? Are you hurting?"

"No, I'm fine," I said. "Did I pass out?"

"No, you just had your eyes closed for about a minute. I'm just worried about why you're jumpy?"

I laid back. "I'm OK," I reassured her, "just had a strange thought." I looked at the clock. "It's almost quarter-to-twelve," I said, "should we just give up?" We agreed to keep the IV in for 10 more minutes, and then be ready for the next series of tests at noon.

I left the hospital just after one o'clock. On the way to my car, I asked myself about the vivid image of Myron. What could it mean? I prayed again that God was preparing me for Myron's recovery. Maybe He was putting it on my heart to be open to welcoming him back with open arms? The image was so clear and unwelcome that it was definitely not my imagination. I had become so afraid of Myron that the last thought on my mind was welcoming him home.

Later that afternoon, my phone rang with a strange number. I sent the call to voicemail. The message was from the Missouri State Highway Patrol's human resource department, and they wanted me to call to discuss Myron. I sighed. I did not want to deal with his drama that afternoon, but I was nervous. Did he jump his probation? Was I in danger?

Shortly afterward, Mason's mom texted me. "Do you know why Myron would be in New York?"

I became hopeful. "Maybe he's in a recovery center?" I responded.

"No, it's not that. People are whispering." Shortly after her response, my phone rang again. This time, I recognized the number. It was a family friend, a local police officer.

"Debra, I don't want to be the one to tell you this, but the Highway Patrol is trying to get in touch with you and I need to let you know before you hear it somewhere else," he said frantically. "Myron jumped off Niagara Falls this afternoon."

I immediately hung up the phone and called the number left on my voicemail. "Are you confirming my husband's death?" I asked. "I am confirming nothing," the voice on the phone responded, "but I am giving you the phone number of a detective in New York who wants to speak with you."

I took the phone with me to my own HR department and closed the door. I sat down as the detective explained to me that eyewitnesses watched Myron remove his boots, then his coat, and jump from an observation bridge into the Niagara River and swim over the American Falls. He was still considered a missing person but presumed dead. Then the detective asked me "why would your husband have left the phone number to the Missouri State Highway Patrol in his hotel room instead of the number to his family? I checked his records and can see that he was a convicted felon. Why would a felon want me to call a police department?"

"Because he isn't actually a felon," I answered, "he was a state trooper for 21 years." I heard the detective's air leave his body. "I understand," he said. "I'll keep you updated as we get more news."

I hung up the phone, and my HR director asked what was going on. "It's over," I said. I felt guilty that I felt some type of relief. "Our nightmare is over. He chose his fate." And with that, I numbly grabbed my things and drove myself home.

According to the online accounts, helicopters were dispatched at 12:50 PM EST to search for a man who had reportedly jumped into the Niagara River.

Myron was missing for ten days. For ten entire days, I sat with friends and family, imagining my husband's body churning over the rocks at the bottom of Niagara Falls. I prayed to him repeatedly to lead investigators to his body. "I can't do anything until you're found," I'd say to him.

The strange part is, Myron was there. He was with us the entire time. Friends would smell his chewing tobacco. Lights on his favorite part of the house would blink incessantly until one of us would call out "we see you, Myron!" Even my dad - the greatest skeptic of all times - reported that he knew Myron was with him when he was cleaning up the shop. I just needed his body to be recovered so that we could go on with our lives.

People called the Niagara Falls Police Department incessantly. Most were not our friends; they were people from our small town, interjecting themselves into our now-public scandal. Some were genuinely concerned about his well-being, but it was still inappropriate behavior at a minimum. Mason retreated to his grandparents' house to stay away from the chatter.

Ten days after Myron jumped, I received the call that his body had been recovered off the coast of Canada. "And, I don't know why I feel compelled to tell you this," the detective added, "but your husband is one tough guy. He didn't have a single broken bone in his body."

When I arrived in New York, the detective walked me through my husband's last moments. He took me to the observation tower to get a bird's eye view of how my husband swam down the center of the Niagara River, to fall to his fate below.

"How long have you been doing this?" I asked.

"A little over 12 years," the detective answered.

"How many people have gone over that waterfall?"

He paused. "Maybe 60-70 a year," he finally answered.

"And how many have broken bones?"

The detective became restless. He finally answered, "all of them."

I turned around to make eye contact. "I believe that God grants special protection to our military and law enforcement," I said. "We send them out to face unspeakable evil, and they carry it. They wear it home every night. They can't always wash it off. But God knows that. I believe he shields them. And Detective, Myron died on the feast of St. Michael the Archangel, the patron saint of law enforcement. I know why my husband didn't have a broken bone. God sent his Archangels to carry him down that waterfall, in one last effort of grace and mercy."

The detective sighed. "You may be right," he said calmly.

I've been told that Myron's doctor had suspected that he suffered from traumatic brain injury. I had inquired numerous times about any work altercations that he may have had in December 2017, when he mysteriously suffered from migraines and before his first seizure, but he refused to acknowledge that this could have been a culprit. In hindsight, I realize how determined he was to keep working and I suspect that he didn't tell me the entire truth.

Mason and I decided to hold off on a funeral until after the holiday season. We were still reeling from the publicity around Myron's death. We knew that a new salacious event would replace his public death, and our small town would move forward from their obsession with Myron's downfall. His

January memorial service was small but beautiful. Just as we had hoped, only those people who truly loved Myron showed up for him. Additionally, Myron's gaming commission colleagues arrived in cars and full uniform - over a dozen of them had made the three-hour drive with their families. We were denied a funeral with honors, so our St. Louis patrol family filled the gap for us.

I spent the months after his death deliberately sitting with my grief. My greatest fears had come true - I was a young widow, and I had lost my dear friend and love of 28 years to his demons. I made the choice to not lose myself to them, too. For the first time in my life, I allowed myself to cry. I accepted that feeling the pain of my loss wasn't going to make me a victim, nor did it make me weak. It just made me a grieving wife. I also gave myself permission to ask for what I needed, when I needed it. If I needed time alone, I took it. If I needed to talk to some-one, I called a friend. Some weekends, my girlfriends would come to my house to keep me company; other weekends I would spend alone hiking or reading. I was cognizant to check in with my family and friends, but I was also clear with them about what I needed.

Six months after Myron's death, I was asked by my suicide support group to tell his story at a law enforcement training event. I immediately said "yes". At first, I thought that I was agreeing for Myron, to continue with his commitment to helping his fellow officers, but upon wrapping up the panel session, I was overcome with the realization that I had done this for me. As I left the stage, I was greeted personally by Javier and Cathy Bustos - the Texas couple that Myron had studied as the blueprint of what he wanted us to do one day. I had inad-vertently fulfilled the destiny that Myron had created for us.

Being a law enforcement family today is difficult. Being a law enforcement suicide widow is isolating. I am fortunate enough to have a strong support system, including fellow LEO suicide survivors. I have had to face every fear I had of being alone, and fight every urge that my underlying codependency may sometimes have. The result has been that I've fallen in love with myself.

I live my life today one day at a time. I find joy in the little moments of my life. I am grateful for my home, my family, my friends, and for just waking up every morning to a new day. I love my solitude. I go to bed every night thanking God for the day, even if that particular day was hard. I wake up each morning grateful that I was able to open my eyes. More and more, I hear from families like mine, families who are suffering in the midst of the chaos of post-traumatic stress disorder and alcoholism. Like me, they feel as though they are suffering alone. I am honored when they share their struggles with me because I understand how much trust they are placing in me, to allow themselves to be honest and vulnerable with me.

I don't know what tomorrow has in store for me. I have faith that God will use me for His glory, that He has created a plan for me that is greater than anything I can imagine. For all of the things that have happened to me, and through all of my own bad decisions, I choose joy. Each time that I doubt my ability to do this, I turn to my life verse, Isaiah 43:1: "Fear not, for I have redeemed you; I have called you by name; you are mine."

ABOUT THE AUTHOR

Debra Downey has overcome the hardships of poverty, abuse, and homelessness to become a successful financial officer and community advocate. She is the daughter of a retired Airman and the widow of a state trooper. Both her mother and her late husband suffered from mental illness, and Debra speaks to groups about the impact this had on her childhood and her marriage.

Debra lives in Missouri with her two German Shepherds. She is currently the Midwest Representative for Survivors of Blue Suicide Foundation, a non-profit group dedicated to supporting the loved ones of law enforcement officers who have died by suicide.

www.ingramcontent.com/pod-product-compliance
Lightning Source LLC
Chambersburg PA
CBHW071323140726
47996CB00005B/1792